BREAK OF A LIFETIME

Micki King

Praise for Micki King and
Break of a Lifetime

"Micki, like thousands of children across the country, grew up spending time with friends at her local YMCA. It was at the Y that Micki first discovered the sport of diving and was encouraged to pursue it competitively. As she perfected her craft, she embraced every challenge and realized her full potential with the help of a supportive community. Throughout her extraordinary life, Micki has made it her mission to pay it forward — inspiring, encouraging, and supporting countless others to reach their full potential."

– Meredith Griffin, Director, Strategy and Quality Practice –
Sports Network Experience, YMCA of the USA

"From being my most ferocious competitor to my hero and best buddy, Micki King has made a lifelong impression on me. Micki distinguished herself on the diving board, in the military, fighting for women's opportunities, and leading all of us who have ever strived for excellence. I wish I could have commented on her amazing preciseness in diving when I worked for television. Micki's journey in this book is one for every age to appreciate."

– Cynthia A. Potter, 28-time USA National Diving Champion,
3-time USA Olympic Diving Team (bronze medalist,
1976 Montreal) and Olympic Diving Analyst for ABC Sports
and NBC Sports for 40 years

"Prepare to be inspired by a true trailblazer and Olympic Champion who became a pioneering advocate for gender equity in sports, the military and in the board room."

– Donna DeVarona, OLY Olympic swimmer
and athlete's rights advocate

"Micki King's athletic journey is legendary and has earned her a position in the U.S Olympic Hall of Fame. However, her accomplishments after her competition accomplishments are just as important for the Olympic and women's sports. The U.S. Air Force was fortunate to have Micki as an officer for more than 25 years."

– Tom Gompf, OLY. Past member USOPC BOD

"Micki King is more than an Olympic Champion; she is a beacon of inspiration and leadership. Her remarkable journey through various careers demonstrates her versatility and commitment to excellence. Micki King's legacy serves as a powerful reminder that greatness is not confined to one arena but can be achieved in all aspects of life. Her example encourages everyone to strive for their best and to lead with integrity and passion."

– Todd Smith, Former Executive Director USA Diving, former President of U.S. Diving Foundation, and former President of Duraflex International

"Consider posing this question in today's society: Should United States Olympians have a voice and a vote in all matters concerning their participation and representation as USA Olympic team members? This book reveals how a courageous group of Olympians sought the respect they deserved, not only on the field of play but also in the boardroom. It offers an incredible insight into the extraordinary life of Olympic Champion Micki King, a role model and inspiration to all who know her."

– Cindy Stinger, U.S. Olympian '84, '88, '92, Executive Director of the Olympians & Paralympians Relief Fund

"Micki and I were a good tennis doubles team, except we both preferred the forehand side. So, we did "paper-scissors-rock" each match, getting laughs from our opponents — until we beat them!"

– Lola Baker, Lexington KY

"Dive into the extraordinary life of Micki King, the female Air Force Captain and 1972 Olympic diving gold medalist, whose inspiring story is a powerful testament to overcoming adversity and achieving lifelong ambitions. This is a must-read for anyone seeking inspiration and/or a deeper understanding of modern Olympic history."

– Bruce Wigo, Olympic historian and former CEO of the International Swimming Hall of Fame

Break of a Lifetime
Author: Micki King
Author: Elaine K. Howley
Editor: Taylor Brien
Proofreader: Lyda Rose Haerle
Research: Timothy Boyle
Cover Design: Nicole Wurtele
Interior Layout: Michael Nicloy

All photographs courtesy of Micki King unless otherwise noted.
Hayes Jones image credit: By International newsreel, public domain.

Special thanks to the International Swimming Hall of Fame, and Heather Martin, Michigan Sports Hall of Fame.

ISBN: 979-8-9913280-5-0

PUBLISHED BY CG SPORTS PUBLISHING

AN IMPRINT OF
NICO 11 PUBLISHING & DESIGN
MUKWONAGO, WISCONSIN
MICHAEL NICLOY, PUBLISHER
www.nico11publishing.com

Quantity order requests can be emailed to:
mike@nico11publishing.com

Printed in The United States of America

Table of Contents

To the friends I've made around the world.

ACKNOWLEDGEMENTS

I would not be the "me" I am today without Coach Dick Kimball. Coach Kimball believed I could be a diving champion and he gave me the chance to prove it. And, yes, there were bumps along the way — as this book recounts. But Coach Kimball knew me better than I knew myself. The Micki King story going forward from my college days would not have happened without Coach Kimball's belief in what I could — and did — achieve.

A special "THANK YOU" to Steve McFarland, a long-time diving buddy, who knows my Olympic journey firsthand. When Steve stepped in to proofread my final chapter, he realized I left out several important details! Having his help at the finish line was so critical. Thank you, thank you again, Steve!!!

FOREWORD

I am deeply honored to have met Micki King as part of my early work with the United States Olympians & Paralympians Association. Micki served as a USOPA board member over many quadrennials. She helped to instill excellence, lead courageously, serve others, and foster belonging among all United States Olympians and Paralympians who competed for the United States at an Olympic & Paralympic Games.

I was young and getting to know all the Olympians who made a significant impact on my understanding of the Olympic Movement, and Micki King was one of those incredible Olympians. A true leader in every sense of the word, she was an Air Force Colonel and a 1972 Diving Gold medalist. Micki played crucial roles in both organizing the first AAC meeting in 1973 and serving as the first Athlete's Advisory Council Chair. Her work on the President's Commission on Olympic Sports led to the passage of the Amateur Sports Act of 1978, giving voice and vote in the governance process of Olympic Sport. It's hard to imagine anything better than that.

Every day, Micki King embodies the Olympic Values, and I am proud to know her. Her leadership has profoundly shaped my own values of service and courage. I remember vividly when Micki shared her insights during a board meeting, inspiring us all to strive for excellence.

Knowing Micki has been one of the greatest honors of my life. Every day, Micki King's dedication to the Olympic Values motivates me to strive for excellence. Thank you, Micki, for being an inspiration and a role model.

Cynthia E. Stinger
U.S. Olympian '84, '88, '92
Executive Director, Olympians & Paralympians Relief Fund

PREFACE

"Miss the beat, you lose the rhythm
And nothing falls into place, no
Only missed by a fraction
Slipped a little off your pace, oh"

— Van Halen, "Right Now"

The damp air barely stirred as I clambered atop the 3-meter diving board at the Alberca Olímpica Francisco Márquez natatorium in Mexico City. More than 4,000 spectators watched in near silence as I placed my feet on the board, set my shoulders, and took a deep breath preparing for the dive to come. I needed that extra moment to ready myself before this dive — a reverse 1½ somersault in the layout position — because it was definitely not my best or favorite dive.

To do this dive, the athlete walks forward to the end of the board but performs the somersault action backward toward the board while keeping the body straight. It requires a strong jump with enough clearance to avoid hitting the board as the somersault "reverses" back toward it.

I had reason to be anxious about this dive. The reverse dives were my weakest group. I had to do this dive eventually, as it was required, but the order I did it in was up to me. Because I was always less confident in the reverse dives, I usually stacked them in the middle of the lineup so I'd have my very best dives to sandwich the routine. Start strong, finish strong.

But here, I had one of my toughest dives toward the end of

the competition. That's how I came to be standing at the back of the 3-meter springboard in the 1968 Olympic Games running through one final mental visualization of how to complete this 9th of 10 dives perfectly.

I felt good standing there, with the clammy air on my skin and the slightest rustling of event programs held by rapt audience members, patiently waiting for me to get on with it. Heading into the finals, I led the pack and had stayed on top for eight dives. The judges, spectators, and other divers knew it was my meet to win or lose.

Gold was close. It was time for me to claim it.

A whiff of chlorine wafted from the pool below as I tilted forward onto the balls of my feet and moved confidently toward the end of the diving board. A split second later, I planted my left foot, just like I had perhaps 10,000 times before. My arms instinctively rose above my head as I bounced skyward. Gravity did what she always does, and both of my feet met tightly together on the board again for that final launch into the take-off for the reverse 1½ somersault in the layout position.

But in that moment as I burst off the board, I knew I was off balance. Diving is a sport of supreme precision. For some reason I'll never fully comprehend, I had not launched outwardly enough from the end of the board. In the time it took me to push off, I understood. I was cooked.

Lady Gravity confirmed that diagnosis as I rotated backwards toward the board. My arms reached over my head again, this time stretching expectantly for the water.

SMACK!

My left forearm hit the very tip of the still-juddering plank, with the stinging thwap of bone against board. I fought the urge to cry out in shock and pain and did my best to hold my form as the water raced up to meet my extended and rapidly numbing fingers.

A mix of searing pain and high-anxiety adrenaline coursed through me as I sank into the cool water. The soothing sensation barely tempered the crushing realization: I'd blown my shot at gold.

I stayed underwater a beat longer than usual, considering my options. My arm ached, and just the thought of hauling myself back onto the tiled deck seemed daunting. Perhaps I could swirl into the drain at the bottom of the pool and forget what just happened?

But my job here wasn't finished yet. There was still one more dive. I had to go on, no matter how much it hurt and regardless of how much I wanted to curl up and cry over the golden opportunity I'd just lost.

Finally, I surfaced and looked to the judges, perched atop tall chairs alongside the pool with their score cards showing 5s and 6s! Wow! I was shocked. I thought the scores would be lower — like 2s!

There's a strange kind of sports math that transpires in moments like these, when your brain — all keyed up from competition and the rush of performing — manages to crunch a complex calculation in a nanosecond. An IBM computer the size of the swimming pool couldn't have added up the judge's scores faster than I did: I instantly knew I'd dropped out of first place. But the judges did not realize I'd hit the board.

So, this wasn't a total loss. I was in trouble, yes. But, if I could pull off a minor miracle on my 10th dive, I might not lose it all. And I did put my best dive last, right?!

Quite simply, if it didn't work, well, it would be an awful way to end my diving career.

CHAPTER 1

SOMETHING IN THE WATER

"The Lake — synonymous with paradise — plays a most important part in the Family Chronicle."

— Lorraine King, Micki's sister

To say I was a tomboy growing up is an understatement. I loved playing outdoors all summer with my cousins, Denny and Richie. My sister Lorraine is four years younger than me, and she always kept up. We four kids were inseparable as youngsters. Denny, Richie, Lorraine, and Maxine — yah!

My given name was Maxine. I'm not sure when I started being called Micki. But I can say for sure, I never felt like a Maxine. I do remember, though, struggling with how to spell my nickname. I had several choices: Mickey, Micky, Mickie, or Micki and no secret now, when I was a teenager, I became Micki. M-I-C-K-I.

Pontiac, Michigan, was my hometown, and it had everything for a kid to love. My special memories were of Lorraine and me playing with our cousins. Their dad and our dad sure knew how to make life fun for us kids. We played baseball, tag, and hide-and-seek all spring and summer. And then we ice skated on local ponds in the winter, playing hockey and tag. Growing up in the "Land of Lakes" was special!

I was a pretty good figure skater and considered it as my primary sport for some time. I even spent two weeks one summer at a figure skating camp at Michigan State University to hone my skills. But figure skating became boring as I pursued it.

Playing in the lake was, for sure, my favorite "sport." My dad and his brother, Uncle Chuck, owned a rustic little cabin on Lotus Lake, and we spent our summers there.

I loved the lake — the sense of being completely free, splashing the water with flippers on, then ducking to chase fish — it was magical. With goggles on my face, I could see a whole other world teeming with fish swimming in seaweed beneath me. I was enchanted.

But this fun ended when autumn pushed summer away and our days at the lake were over 'til next year. There was nothing to do indoors that occupied me for more than 15 minutes. I drove my folks crazy all winter. When I turned 10, my mom learned the local YMCA had girls' day twice a week at their indoor pool. Suddenly, I was swimming at the Y when it was snowing outdoors! Yippee!

It was fun to be back in the water, but by comparison to the lake, the indoor pool seemed downright boring. I missed chasing fish, and I wasn't all that interested in looking at the pool's concrete bottom. But swimming indoors in the depth of winter, when the lake was frozen, was better than sitting at home. It was still boring… but there was that diving board.

Every Tuesday and Thursday on girls' day, we'd challenge each other to cannonballs and other tricks and flips off the diving board. I'd end up back at home, exhausted and bleary-eyed from the chlorine but grinning ear to ear. It was all about fun and just being a kid.

So, my diving career started as innocent play. Horsing around with friends on the diving board at the Pontiac YMCA was pure fun and not available to me at the lake. That was the initial enticement. And over time, I discovered I liked flipping and twisting off the boards. Eventually, I started trying new tricks and flips just to see if I could do them.

When I was 14, the lifeguard at the pool was named JL LaMont. He had been a diver in high school. One day when I was flipping off the board, he came over to me.

"You're pretty good at that, you know," he said with a smile.

I shrugged. "Flips are fun!" I grinned, as water streamed down my face and pooled on the tiles under my feet.

"But, that's not a flip. That's a front somersault tuck," he said.

"A what?" I asked.

"A front somersault tuck. It's an easy dive and a key starting point to learn the more difficult dives," he said.

That sure got my attention. Of course I wanted to know more. "What do you mean?" I asked.

"Well, if you just tuck a little tighter when you leave the board, you can probably add another half a somersault to your dive," he gestured toward the board.

"How do I do that?" I asked.

And thus began my first diving lesson.

When JL approached, I was blissfully unaware of what lay ahead, and I had no inkling then that diving would soon open many doors in my future. At the time, I just wanted to learn how to do more somersaults and twists than the boys did. So

I listened carefully to everything JL told me. I practiced, and practiced, and practiced, and before long, I had several solid dives in my repertoire.

As I continued working with JL, I developed into a not-half-bad diver. But I often think back on that moment when he first reached out to offer assistance. If JL hadn't been the lifeguard on duty that year and if he hadn't had the inclination to help me, I would have missed out on diving altogether, and I'm not the me I am today.

It amazes me to think how that single interaction changed my life.

But finding opportunities to continue diving and expanding my skills in the sport became challenging as I grew older. At the time, there were no formal high school or college sports for girls — this was the late 1950s, long before the passage of Title IX would require opportunities for female athletes. At the time, only the Amateur Athletic Union (the AAU) hosted competitions for girls, and when I had enough dives that met the requirements of competitive diving, JL signed me up for one of those AAU meets.

That's when I realized this diving stuff was becoming serious business. It was no longer just about going to the Y and playing with my friends. It was about competition and pride and so many other things that really appealed to me. But those things also induced some anxiety. Diving had started to become a piece of my identity.

Suddenly, the stakes had shot up and I got nervous. I felt the pressure of it not just being a flip. Now it was a "front somersault tuck" and people were going to look at what I was doing and judge me and my skills. From how well I pointed my toes, to the splash on my entry, it suddenly all mattered a whole lot.

But my ability pushed diving into a new dimension for me. I thrived off that energy and the anticipation of competition.

And, by the way, I won that first meet.

I grew up in Pontiac in the post-World War II decades of the '40s and '50s. Nearby Detroit was riding the high of the automobile era and the prosperity that came from peace in Europe and mechanical innovation at home.

At the time, Detroit was easily one of the most important cities in the United States — the home of Motown and America's love affair with the automobile. And this access to security and opportunity reverberated in many ways throughout my life, including the chance to attend good schools and take ice skating lessons. But the proximity to Detroit would also make my diving career escalate going forward.

I recently came across a book about Pontiac that relates the history of the city, which was founded in 1818. The town grew up on a plot of land about 30 miles north of Detroit and was named for Pontiac, the warrior chief of the Ottawa Nation, who had led the "Indian Uprising" of 1763 against the British at Fort Detroit and Fort Michilimackinac. In time, Pontiac became a mill town, railroad hub, wagon-and-buggy manufacturing center, the site of a state asylum, and of course, a mecca for the automobile industry. Pontiac churned out untold numbers of buses and trucks before and during the heyday of General Motors Truck & Coach Division, and in 1928, with the building of the Pontiac Municipal Airport, the city's status as a key hub of innovation and industry was sealed.

In some senses, what Pontiac did for the auto industry, it also did for me and my diving. Early on, it was Pontiac's proximity to Detroit that allowed me to see diving first-hand at the highest level. The 1960 Olympic Trials were held in Detroit at Brennan Pools, a large complex with two main pools and a diving area with two 3-meter springboards and a 10-meter tower, located about 20 miles from Pontiac. I was 16 years old then, and at the time, athletes didn't have to qualify for the Trials. I could just turn up and try out. So, I went to see how I'd do. Why not, right?

Little did I anticipate the huge challenge ahead of me.

At warm-ups a week before the Trials in Detroit, I got in line with other divers taking their turns. But, I had only dived from

a 1-meter board — that was all they had at the Y — so this move to the higher 3-meter board was a HUGE difference for me. Going from the Y's 3-foot high board to Olympic diving's 3-meter high springboard — that's 10 feet above the water — was scary for me.

At these Trials in 1960, the athletes coached each other, including me as I stood in line with them. And, they were generous to me with their feedback. One of the divers told me, "Your hurdle needs to be a little longer," and then another would applaud a good dive and offer additional feedback about my entry or body angle. It all seemed way less about competing against each other, and more about working out together.

I didn't know any of these divers, but they were all very nice to help me as they did. This went on for the week leading up to Trials.

Five of the seven prelim dives were "easy" ones, like the jack-knife, for instance, which JL had taught me at the Y. And, I managed to successfully do the jack-knife dive from the 3-meter in Detroit without getting hurt. As the other divers coached me, I was starting to feel good.

Undeterred, I entered the 1960 Olympic Trials. The practice sessions motivated me as the other divers gave me positive feedback. They seemed impressed with my dives. Flattered, hugely encouraged, and with my ego inflating generously, I believed every word they said.

At some point during proceedings — fueled by all the "good jobs!" and pats on the back I was getting after each dive — I realized that if I made finals, I'd have to perform three more optional dives that I had never even tried before. I knew I couldn't do them even in my dreams!

But, the other divers were so encouraging, I began to believe I could actually make finals — and I started to worry about what to do if that happened. How could I possibly fake three dives that I hadn't learned yet?

I finally voiced this concern at a practice session and was met with several awkward smiles. Finally, one of them said, "Micki, I don't know how to tell you this, but you don't need to worry. You're not going to make the finals."

The other divers seemed relieved that this one guy had told me the truth. I was embarrassed that I had gotten so ahead of myself. I realized they were right. There was no way I was going to make finals — at the U.S. Olympic Trials, no less — and to even think this so early in my journey was a bit silly.

As it turned out, I finished 29th out of 30 divers entered in the Trials. At least I wasn't last, right?

But looking back, it was the support and kindness I received in the 1960 Olympic Trials in Detroit that propelled me to keep going, to work harder, and to not give up. I kept diving in the AAU events and steadily got better. Before long, I was consistently a top performer in my AAU age group.

It took a lot of hard work. Diving became a major part of every day. Just like eating breakfast, I went to workout daily. It became part of me, an identity, and I loved every minute of it.

My high school days in Pontiac were great. I had no idea what was ahead for me—but who does, right? I was good at diving, and eager to keep winning those AAU medals. And it turned out I wasn't the only Pontiac High School student that was in two Olympics.

Hayes Jones was a phenomenal runner who won the 110-meter hurdles at the Tokyo Olympics in 1964 *and* earned a bronze medal in Rome in 1960! He was six years older than me, so I didn't overlap with him during high school, but I was well aware of him. (Though we didn't know each other in high school, we've since connected and stay in touch regularly.)

It's pretty incredible to think that two Olympic champions hailed from the same working-class town in southeastern Michigan. That humble factory city just north of Detroit didn't have a big population to draw from, and Pontiac didn't exactly have world-class athletic facilities or coaches to develop local talent. So to produce two Olympic champions — in two different sports — in such a short span of time is remarkable.

It also gives me chills to think that I'd walked the halls of an Olympic champion well before my own Olympic dreams would come to fruition. It's uncanny, and it really makes me wonder, what was so special about that small corner of America at that particular time in history?

This connection also underscores that America is a land of opportunity. Even a tough, northern factory city can produce an extraordinary and improbable outcome — twice — when the right factors converge.

CHAPTER 2

EXPANDING HORIZONS

"The best protection a woman can have is courage."

— Elizabeth Cady Stanton, prominent 19th century leader of the women's rights movement and an early advocate for women's suffrage

When it came time for college, I had my heart set on Michigan State. But that's not what my parents had in mind. They had already enrolled me at the University of Michigan.

I really didn't want to go to UM. And when I say I didn't want to go, I mean, I *really* didn't want to go. All my friends from high school were headed off to Michigan State, and I was the only one going to the University of Michigan.

But my parents were adamant that Michigan was the best option for me; they knew Michigan had a renowned diving coach and Michigan State had no coach. So, if I wanted to fulfill my potential as a diver, I needed to go to Michigan. I disagreed, preemptively mourning all the parties and fun times I'd miss with my friends who would be at Michigan State. But Mom and

Dad laid down the law. I was going to Michigan and that was that. They packed up the car and we drove to Ann Arbor.

So I did the only thing I could in that moment to protest: I cried the whole way.

But something special happened when we pulled up to my dorm. A handsome football dude reached out to open my door. It was something the football team did for the incoming freshman girls. That small act caught my 17-year-old, slightly boy-crazed attention, and the tears quieted.

A few moments later, that same guy helped me move everything into my dorm room. He was tall and broad and had a great smile. Suddenly, I knew Michigan was the right place for me!

While that footballer may have caught my eye, it wasn't his sports career I was interested in. It was my own, and Michigan offered me a unique opportunity at the time — the chance to train with Dick Kimball, one of the best diving coaches in the world.

But the catch was — women's collegiate athletics did not exist at the time. The pool at Michigan was solely the domain of the men's team, and I did not qualify to use it for obvious reasons.

In 1962 when I arrived on campus, the passage of the Sex Equity in Education Act, better known as Title IX, was still a decade up the road. And I'll say it again, there simply were no sports opportunities for women at the high school and collegiate level, and women were limited to competing within the AAU.

But at the University of Michigan, I had a coach willing to train me for AAU events and help me qualify for the Olympic Games. Coach Kimball was willing to do all that, but he did so at significant risk to his own job.

✶ ✶ ✶

While at first I might not have been super thrilled about attending Michigan, I quickly discovered that training with Dick Kimball was exactly what I needed. Coach Kimball was a legend in the sport by the 1960s for his own skills as a diver. But he'd achieved even more acclaim for his coaching prowess and his innovative approach to training and competition.

Perhaps Coach Kimball's biggest contribution to the sport came when he invented the trampoline spotting rig, which plays a major part to this day in helping generations of divers learn to execute new dives safely. The rig consists of a harness attached to a pulley system; the diver straps into the harness while the coach counterweights the other end of the rigging. Then, the athlete can bounce and spin using the trampoline to their heart's content, without fear of landing wrong or getting injured.

That rigging system represented a giant leap forward in training safety from diving boards mounted over the sandpits of old. Coach Kimball's trampoline and spotting rig soon started popping up on pool decks all around the country. Coach Kimball even got Johnny Carson to try the spotting rig and trampoline when he and I appeared on *The Tonight Show Starring Johnny Carson* in 1972.

Coach Kimball was also well known for staging funny, acrobatic diving exhibitions with another superlative diver and extraordinary coach, Hobie Billingsley, who coached the Indiana University team. Over the years, as Coach Kimball and Coach Billingsley introduced the trampoline around the country, it soon became a staple of diver training. Today, every diving program uses a trampoline and spotting rig to help divers learn new moves.

My parents understood well that given Coach Kimball's expertise and connections, he was the best coach for me. He was a true pioneer and an innovator and exactly the mentor I needed. Coach Kimball was way ahead of his time, in both his coaching knowledge and his support of female athletes. Again, we're talking the early and mid-1960s, many years before Title IX would make women's athletics commonplace in high school and college. But a decade earlier, Coach Kimball allowed me to work out with the men's team.

I can remember a few times when the athletic director would pop into the natatorium to chat with the swim coach, Gus Stager. The AD would stay for a couple of minutes to watch the men work out. Of course, I wasn't supposed to be in the men's pool, so at the first sign of the AD, I would jump into the water and duck down below the gutter in the diving well — the farthest point away from the door. I was literally hiding. I was lucky the athletic director never actually came over to the diving well to talk to Coach Kimball or I for sure would have been discovered and who knows what kind of trouble that would cause. The rules were clear: Women were not allowed in the "men's" pool.

I was also lucky that Gus totally supported Coach Kimball. Perhaps it was because Coach Stager was involved with the Olympic movement — he was the swimming coach for the 1960 U.S. Olympic Team — and he understood there were bigger things to worry about than whether women were training with the men in Michigan. In any event, he could have easily turned me in, but he never breathed a word about my working out in the men's pool, and the AD remained blissfully unaware. Thus, I was able to train with a great coach at a great facility while I got a great college education. A win-win-win to be sure.

Coach Kimball understood I loved diving and allowed me to train there and become the best diver I could be. I'm also grateful that my parents understood from the beginning that Coach Kimball was the coach I needed.

It's amazing to me when I think back how progressive my parents were, but also, that Coach Kimball believed in my abilities and supported my becoming an elite diver. At the time, there were so few opportunities for female athletes, I had only one or two role models to look up to. It would have been easy to miss my chance all together if I didn't have a supportive family and great coaching along the way.

Coach Stager and Coach Kimball developed excellent teams. Michigan won the NCAA National Swimming and Diving Championships four times with them at the helm, and some of the best swimmers and divers in the country funneled through Michigan over two and a half decades. The Michigan team continues to be one of the very best swimming and diving programs in the country today. Gus Stager and Dick Kimball left a deep legacy at the school and in aquatic sports overall.

I played a small part in that history by "sneaking" into the pool. And this made it possible for Coach Kimball to help me climb the AAU ladder.

Over the course of my career, I earned 10 AAU diving titles. In 1972 when I earned my ninth title, I was 27 years old, and the Associated Press referred to me as "Mamma Max" because I was considered old. (How did they even know I was once "Maxine?") But, I suppose it was better than the commentary the AP reported in 1967 on another AAU title I won in the one-meter springboard event. Then, I was described as "a blonde cutie whose svelte figure belies her status as a U.S. Air Force Lieutenant." Times were different then and journalistic standards have certainly changed, but I was always more interested in winning than in what the press said about anything I did or their judgment of how I looked.

In addition to winning AAU Nationals 10 times, I was named diver of the year in 1965, 1969, and 1972 in the springboard, and in 1969 in the platform diving event. And it all started while I was training with Dick Kimball at the University of Michigan.

Since those days at Michigan, more than 50 years ago, a lot

has changed in the world of women's sports. Today, access for women to play sports at all levels is a federal law. But it didn't happen without a fight, and the push for full parity continues today. My generation started that movement, and I'm pleased that I've worked with and been friends with many of these pioneers for decades.

One of these amazing women is Olympic swimming champion Donna de Varona. She won her gold medal at the Tokyo Olympics in 1964 at the tender age of 17. She dominated her sport on the world stage, but because there were no sports for girls when she was a teenager, Donna never once competed for her high school or college.

Another key early advocate for women's sports was Billie Jean King, one of the greatest tennis players to ever grace the sport. She won 39 Grand Slam titles and a slew of other tournaments and titles between 1960 and 1980. She was the first female athlete ever to be named *Sports Illustrated* Sportsman of the Year, which occurred in 1972. Her career prize money winnings reached nearly $2 million.

An amazing tennis player, Billie Jean has also long been a visionary leader in the quest for inclusion and equity. Just a few of her landmark efforts include successfully lobbying for equal pay for women at the 1973 U.S. Open, founding the Women's Tennis Association, and founding the Women's Sports Foundation, which continues to push for girls and women to have access to sporting opportunities. Billie Jean's contributions to social change and equity have been so enormous and enduring that in 2009, then-President Obama presented her with the Presidential Medal of Freedom. And the tennis gear she wore to beat Bobby Riggs during the famous 1973 "Battle of the Sexes" (more on that later) is on display at the National Museum of American History.

I digress. But I mention this all because this historical context is important to being able to recognize where women's sports were when I was in college and how that compares to where they are today. Women like Donna, Billie Jean, and I encountered many roadblocks and frustrating hoops we had to jump through to gain any access at all to the playing field. This is part of what makes it so gratifying to see athletes like Megan Rapinoe, who led the U.S. Women's Soccer team to World Cup glory in 2015 and 2019, gain pay parity with the U.S. Men's Soccer team. These women have finally achieved the equity my generation could only dream of. Their success reminds me that, even though it's still a work in progress, our struggles were not in vain. We pushed the envelope and we helped precipitate change for the women who followed.

We had to start somewhere, and it's been a lifelong honor to help give today's women a boost as they chase their own dreams.

I don't think it's overstating it to compare the development of women's sports at the collegiate level to the fight for women's suffrage. In 1920, after many years of struggle, American women finally got the right to vote. Yet, 46 years later, I was hiding from the athletics director at the University of Michigan when he stopped by swim practice, because women weren't allowed in the men's pool. A straight line can be drawn from one event to the other.

Thankfully times have changed, but that progress hasn't had a strictly linear trajectory.

Much of the progress we've seen over the past five decades has been related to the passage of Title IX. In just 37 words, that law established a legal right for women to gain access to athletic and educational opportunities on every college campus in the United States that takes federal funding.

The law states:

"No person in the United States shall, on the basis of sex, be excluded from participation in, be denied the benefits of, or be subjected to discrimination under any education program or activity receiving Federal financial assistance."

Sounds great, right? It was revolutionary, to be sure. But despite its still being an enforceable, federal law on the books today, many colleges are not in compliance!

There is real data to back this up. According to a 2022 *USA Today* report, a whopping 87% of NCAA Division I football bowl subdivision schools do not offer athletic opportunities to women in proportion to their enrollment, as the federal law requires!

Two years later, in May 2024, the U.S. Government Accountability Office confirmed that federal gender-equity laws related to college athletics are systematically violated and effectively unenforced. The GAO report found that 93% of universities had female athletic participation rates lower than their enrollment rate while 63% of schools had participation-enrollment gaps of 10% or wider. Across the board, the athletic participation rate for collegiate women was 14% less than their enrollment rate. Clearly, there's an imbalance, but no school has yet been sued by the federal government or had their funding pulled for being noncompliant with Title IX.

While those figures are shocking, there's more to Title IX than proportionality; it's just one of three ways to test for compliance with Title IX. The other two relate to expansion of opportunities and accommodation of "interests and ability" of the underrepresented sex.

Those other two measures are harder to quantify than enrollment proportionality, and enforcement gets messy quickly given the cost variables between big men's sports like football versus smaller sports like women's volleyball. Smaller teams that need less equipment require less funding, so the calculus can get complicated. In short, there's a lot of nuance involved when assessing whether a particular school is truly in compliance. But the point is, **the work of Title IX isn't finished yet.**

Still, Title IX most certainly has changed the landscape for female collegiate athletes over the past 50 years. Back when I was in school, there simply was no playing field for women. But now, female athletes have vastly more opportunities, and in some places, those options are on par with what men can access. This exciting evolution toward equity and equality began with my generation.

At the time, I didn't think of my diving with the men at Michigan in the 1960s as a form of protest; I was just a diver wanting to train and compete to achieve my highest potential. And Coach Kimball was totally on board to help me become the best diver I could be.

But I suppose, looking back, you could cast it as an act of rebellion — a pushing back against the powers-that-were or even society as a whole. I simply loved to dive and wanted to be better at it, and I'm so glad that I found a like-minded mentor in Coach Kimball when I arrived at the University of Michigan.

A reporter once asked Coach Kimball for a quote after I had won an AAU title. The question to him was, "How does it feel to coach a woman to a National Championship?"

Coach Kimball's answer was, "I don't coach men, and I don't coach women. I coach people!"

CHAPTER 3

AN EQUAL OPPORTUNITY

"You were born with potential. You were born with goodness and trust. You were born with ideals and dreams. You were born with greatness. You were born with wings. You are not meant for crawling, so don't. You have wings. Learn to use them and fly."

— Rumi, 13th-century Persian Sufi mystic, poet, and theologian

I'm not sure exactly when I realized women made less money than men in most professions, even when doing the exact same work, side-by-side. But, I immediately knew I wasn't interested in participating in that sort of system. If I was going to work, and give it my all, then I was going to earn the same as any man doing the same job. It was that simple.

Sadly, there weren't many jobs where women were guaranteed to make the same money as their male counterparts. But the military had gender pay parity. I went for an interview, and the recruiter confirmed I'd be paid the same as every man at my rank. And, he told me about the Air Force sports program that supported athletes with Olympic potential. That's what I needed to hear, so the next day I signed up!

As the recruiter promised, my first duty was on staff of the Air Force ROTC detachment on the Michigan campus. This

meant I was able to continue training with Coach Kimball — as an Air Force lieutenant now!

Going into the military turned out to be a dream job. I worked in that initial position with the ROTC detachment at Michigan between 1966 and 1968, and I was able to establish a great training routine that would carry me to my first Olympic Games. In addition to equal pay for equal work and employment security, I was able to continue training.

My work schedule was very stable, so I could plan my training like clockwork. It wasn't easy, though; this was my first duty as an Air Force officer, and I was a rookie. I knew that meant extra scrutiny. So I went out of my way to be early to every meeting. I was always sure my uniform was pressed and in line with the standards. I did my best every single day so I didn't draw any negative attention to myself.

With that discipline and determination, I continued diving. I'd begin my Air Force ROTC workday at 7 a.m., then I'd go to the pool on my lunch break from 12 to 1 p.m. During that mid-day workout, I'd stretch, lift weights, and complete my dryland work. When I was finished, I'd go back on duty from 1 until 5 p.m. After my Air Force ROTC workday ended, I'd complete a second workout from 5 to 6:30 p.m. in the pool — diving, diving, diving.

My Air Force job was fairly routine, and my diving fit in without any problem — most of the time. I thrived on the orderly, regimented schedule. Summers were slow with cadets on break from school, which made it easier to travel for competitions. It really was the perfect situation for me to continue building my diving skills after college. Without the Air Force, I'm not sure I could have kept training to compete in the 1968 Olympics.

I fully intended to retire from diving after those Games in Mexico. At that point in time, athletes typically competed in just one Olympics. The Olympics were strictly amateur back then, unlike today where athletes can make a living as a professional swimmer, runner, soccer player... Back then, there were strict rules that forbade the earning of money by athletes who intended to retain Olympic eligibility. This rule changed in 1986 but was still firmly in place when I was competing.

Because of those strictures, most athletes were not able to support themselves while training at the elite level. Usually after one Olympics, they moved on to the next chapter of their lives.

Again, this is why the Air Force had been so clutch for me. I had work and duties to discharge for the Air Force, but they were well aware that I was a potential Olympic athlete. As an athlete-member of the Air Force Elite Sports Program, I got support from the Air Force in exchange for my representing the United States in international competition. The better I did, the better America did in the eyes of the world, so it was truly a win-win collaboration. They supported me, and I was thrilled to be part of it.

The Vietnam War was raging, so when the Games were over, I fully expected to be reassigned and deployed to the war zone.

I did get orders for duty in Southeast Asia. And unsurprisingly, when I received the notice, I did feel some anxiety about what I might face overseas. But I was an Air Force officer and it was my turn. Really, I felt very at peace with leaving diving behind me.

But of course, it didn't work out that way. Life seldom does what you expect it to. And for me, it was all because of diving.

CHAPTER 4

HIGH STAKES AT HIGH ALTITUDE

"Close only counts in horseshoes and hand grenades."

— Frank Robinson, Major League Baseball player and manager

Held August 21st through 24th in Long Beach, California, the 1968 Olympic Trials brought serious pressure. The U.S. Olympic Trials in most sports are more intense than the Olympic Games themselves because the competition is so fierce for few slots on the American squad. Just getting to the Olympics is an enormous accomplishment anywhere, but in a large nation like America where there's a deep pool of talent, simply making the team carries even more weight.

It was no different in 1968 when I walked onto the deck of the Belmont Plaza Olympic pool to face off against several women I knew were incredibly talented contenders for the three coveted slots in the springboard, and three in the platform diving events.

The competition was so tight that the 1968 U.S. Olympic

Team coach, Hobie Billingsley, commented afterward to *Swimming World* magazine that "the pressure here was as much as you could ask. It was so thick, you couldn't see anything." Scoring eights on all your dives might be enough to keep you in contention, but even that wasn't certain; there were absolutely no gimmies to be had. All of the women, including Lesley Bush, the 1964 Gold medalist on the platform, had beaten me in AAU meets over the years. I knew I had to bring my A-game.

I also knew my chance of qualifying in the 10-meter platform diving event wasn't as strong as in the 3-meter springboard. I was comfortable on the platform and had won Nationals once, too, but my springboard dives were always that little bit better. I focused on the 3-meter. This was a good strategy, since I didn't make the finals in the platform event at Olympic Trials.

But even in the 3-meter springboard, there was no assurance I would make the cut. Things started rough as I gutted it out through the required dives. But over the course of the meet, I rose from eighth place to finish in second place with a total of 405.06 points. I finished behind Keala O'Sullivan of Hawaii, who notched 447.90 for first place, and ahead of Sue Gossick of California, who had finished fourth at the 1964 Games. Gossick nearly missed her shot at making the '68 team when she hit the board on one of her optional dives and dropped out of the lead position. But ever the cool customer, she recovered and punched her ticket to Mexico City. She would be a formidable challenger south of the border in October.

When all was said and done, I was relieved to have secured an Olympic berth. As much as I wanted to win the event outright, when making a team is at stake, that takes precedence. Second place was good enough to ensure I'd get to Mexico, where first would count far more. As challenging as it was to simply be one of the top three in the United States, I was more interested in being the best in the world.

From the moment Trials ended, I focused on one thing:

nabbing the gold medal in Mexico. To meet that aim, Coach Kimball helped me concentrate on consistency in training to make sure I'd be ready when the time came.

Still, I was very aware that I was mostly a rookie. Up until that point, I had only left the state of Michigan a few times, and had done no international traveling. Going to Mexico not to vacation but as a representative of the United States at the Olympic Games — well that was knock-your-socks-off remarkable to me. It was now my turn to fly, and I was so excited for it. I had roughly two months to prepare. I was ready to get back to work, and Coach Kimball was there for me.

Suddenly, I was on an airplane headed to Colorado Springs, Colorado. "Why there?" you ask. Easy answer — sort of!

Mexico City sits at an altitude of 7,349 feet, so the air is "thin" at that height and "thin" air is an issue for athletes in peak condition — especially runners and swimmers. So the pre-Olympic training site was at the Air Force Academy pool in Colorado, located in the Rocky Mountains at 7,258 feet — almost exactly bang-on what we'd be facing in Mexico!

Of course, altitude is not the issue for divers that it is for swimmers. But both squads trained together that year and it was all good. Now, here I was, suddenly out of Michigan in Colorado on my way to Mexico City.

Today, most Team USA swimmers travel to the U.S. Olympic & Paralympic Training Center in Colorado Springs for altitude training at least once a year as part of their training regimen. But it wasn't a tradition yet when I came along. Our group was the first that really needed to acclimate to high altitudes to be competitive, and that was because of Mexico City's elevation. But our experience got the ball rolling for creating the annual practice that future Olympians would also travel to Colorado for altitude training.

While training, I was surrounded by the women I wanted to

beat in Mexico. It was a strange situation to be part of the same team while also being in direct competition with each other. This was an awkward situation, but unavoidable given the nature of our sport. I found I spent more time with the swimmers than the other divers.

In a blink, it was time to board the plane to Mexico City. When we landed, I couldn't shake the thought this was all too much to believe. Here I was, a girl from a factory town up north, setting foot in a thriving Latin metropolis to represent my country at the Olympic Games. To say it was a dream come true would be trite; it was a dream alright, but I hoped I would not wake up before I saw how it all turned out.

As exciting as it was to be in Mexico City at that moment, like anything in life, it wasn't perfect. Several obstacles had arisen on the road to the Olympic Games, and looking back, I realize it was a small miracle it came together and the 1968 Olympic Games transpired at all.

The Games were held from October 12 to October 27, 1968, in the midst of one of the most historically significant years in human history. In short, the world was on fire. The Soviets had just invaded Prague, squelching the hopeful reform movement known as the Prague Spring and deepening the Cold War's divide between East and West. The Vietnam War was in full swing and the Tet Offensive, a major escalation of the conflict launched by the Viet Cong and the North Vietnamese, had only recently come to a bloody conclusion after nine months of horrific fighting. The U.S. had lost many troops and had sunk all but irretrievably into the quagmire.

Things at home weren't much better; in response to the Vietnam War, student protests abounded in America — with vast reverberations abroad — and the assassination of Martin Luther

King Jr. at a Memphis hotel in April 1968 stoked civil unrest. The assassination of Robert F. Kennedy just two months later at a hotel in Los Angeles added to the upheaval, and the Civil Rights Movement hit a fever pitch as Black Americans demanded their rights. To think the Olympic flame could actually be lit peacefully among all this turmoil was difficult to fathom.

Despite its best efforts to rise above political and social conflict, the Olympic organization was unable to distance itself from the generational conflict surging all around it, especially as Black American athletes threatened a boycott of the Games to bring attention to their struggles at home.

One such effort, the Olympic Project for Human Rights, had been founded in 1967 by Harry Edwards, a former San Jose State College discus thrower and basketball player who sought to bring athletes together to support the fight for equal rights. Edwards formed a coalition of prominent Black American athletes, including fellow San Jose State track superstars Tommie Smith and John Carlos, to draw attention to the plight of Black athletes and the institutionalized racism they faced in America. Using such slogans as "Why run in Mexico and crawl at home?" the OPHR threatened a boycott of the Games in protest of the poor treatment Black athletes received in the U.S.

Hearing the call for Black athletes to boycott, Kareem Abdul-Jabbar, then known as Lew Alcindor and already one of the most popular and talented basketball players ever to grace the game, declared he wouldn't try out for the Olympic team. The movement gathered steam, and the OPHR garnered the attention of Dr. Martin Luther King Jr. who understood that sports and Black athletes' skills and growing platform within professional and Olympic athletics, would be key to changing the narrative about what it meant to be Black in America. Edwards and King met in Manhattan, and King endorsed the OPHR, supporting the group's efforts to boycott the Olympics.

The OPHR had four strategic demands. The first was the

reinstatement of Muhammad Ali's heavyweight boxing title, of which he'd been stripped in 1966 when declaring himself a conscientious objector to the Vietnam War and refusing to be drafted into the U.S. Army to serve in Southeast Asia. The OPHR also demanded South Africa and Southern Rhodesia — two countries that openly practiced Apartheid, an extreme system of race segregation — be banned from the Games. And they demanded more African American coaches be hired to work with the U.S. Olympic teams.

The group's most important demand was for the removal of Avery Brundage (an American track athlete who'd competed in the 1912 Olympics and became an administrator) from the chairmanship of the International Olympic Committee. Brundage had been the only non-European to ascend to the top leadership position within the IOC until June 2025, when Kirsty Coventry, a Zimbabwean Olympic swimmer became the new IOC president (remarkable for many reasons, not least of which because she is the first African and first woman to assume the leadership role). A controversial figure, Brundage, who served as the fifth president of the organization from 1952 until 1972, fought against a proposed boycott of the 1936 Summer Olympics in Berlin, then controlled by Adolf Hitler and his Nazi political machine. In short, Brundage had made clear he harbored some less-than sympathetic attitudes towards Jews, Blacks, and other minorities.

While the OPHR was not successful in having Brundage removed, nor in restoring Muhammad Ali's heavyweight boxing title, the high-profile press the movement received did result in some changes. They were successful in getting South Africa and Southern Rhodesia banned from the Games, and a handful of Black coaches were brought onto the U.S. Olympic team's roster. In response to these changes, and the fallout of Dr. King's assassination, the OPHR quieted their calls for a boycott. But the group left open the possibility of some other action at the Games.

Meanwhile, the host city had some big challenges of its own to work through. The Games were to be held in up-and-coming Mexico City, a sprawling and prosperous settlement of some 8 million people at the time. This was the first time the Games would travel to a Spanish-speaking country, and not everyone was happy about it. On October 2, 1968, just 10 days before the Olympics were set to open, a massive student protest took place in the Plaza de las Tres Culturas, a large square about 15 miles from the as-yet-uncompleted Olympic Village. Thousands of students turned out to peacefully demonstrate against the government of then-President Gustavo Diaz Ordaz Bolaños and the upcoming Olympic Games, which they felt were a huge distraction from their push for revolution.

In an instant, what started as a peaceful action turned deadly, with some 300 to 400 people being massacred. The Mexican press asserted that the students opened fire on soldiers who'd been sent in to shut down the protest. I had no knowledge that this had transpired just days before I arrived in Mexico — it took years for the full story to emerge. Documents declassified many years later indicated that snipers — members of an elite team assembled as part of the safety precautions for the Games and positioned around the plaza at the behest of President Ordaz — opened fire. It seems the whole affair was staged to make it look like civilians started the volley, but it was an elaborate plan to justify the government's desire to crush the students' anti-authoritarian movement. The government did its best to literally whitewash the tragedy by painting the plaza white to cover the blood stains left by those who'd died. The aim was to hide the incident from the rest of the world before everyone arrived for the quadrennial festival that aims to foster world peace and understanding.

Suffice it to say, the Games were on rocky footing before they started. But the organizers certainly did one thing right — they had Enriqueta Basilio, a Mexican hurdler, light the torch at the opening. It was the first time in history that a woman lit the Olympic cauldron.

With all that turbulence in the background — of which I was blissfully unaware — Mexico opened its doors to athletes from around the world. But the controversies didn't end when the competition started. The most memorable of these, of course, was the infamous Black Power salute made by track stars Tommie Smith and John Carlos when they stood atop the podium for winning gold and bronze in the men's 200-meter sprint. They stood quietly for 80 seconds — in just their socks to signify the poverty so many Black people in America endure — with heads bowed as the "Star-Spangled Banner" played throughout the massive stadium. Each wore a single, black leather glove on a raised fist. That silent statement, condemned by many, nevertheless drew the world's attention to their position that the Civil Rights Movement in America hadn't gone far enough.

Afterward Smith and Carlos, who had been involved with the OPHR, told reporters that "all we ask for is an equal chance to be a human being." This enduring image is just one of many memorable elements of a dynamic Olympic Games that played out against the backdrop of a rapidly changing world.

I didn't meet Tommie or John in Mexico, and I don't think I even knew about the protest when it first happened. But when I heard about it afterwards and how upset so many people were, I was bewildered. Why shouldn't these athletes — among the very best in the world — take advantage of the global stage they had earned the right to stand atop to draw attention to their cause? I completely supported them and that peaceful action and couldn't imagine what they'd gone through for that.

I had grown up in a racially mixed community. My dad worked alongside many Black men and women, and my first diving coach, JL LaMont, was Black. Without these terrific members of our community, where would I have ended up? Certainly not in Mexico City for my first Olympic Games.

I just couldn't understand why people were so up in arms about these young men asking that their human rights be respected. They were using their voice in a meaningful way, and that's something that would stick with me for the rest of my life.

But that was all to come in the future. When I tuned up at my first and presumed only Olympic Games, I had very different concerns on my mind. For starters, the coach of the U.S. Women's Diving squad in Mexico was Hobie Billingsley, the diving coach at Michigan's Big 10 rival, Indiana University. My coach Dick Kimball and Coach Billingsley were best friends, but also big rivals!

They coached against each other in Big 10 dual meets and they recruited against each other, too; each worked hard to convince incoming freshmen that "his" school was the better option.

Coach Billingsley was picked as the 1968 Olympic diving coach, and I was good with it. I liked and respected Coach Billingsley — and for good reason. I knew Coach Billingsley and was comfortable with him, and I knew Coach Kimball would bring him up to speed about my diving — my strengths and weaknesses and advice I needed during this competition.

So, Coach Billingsley was not a stranger to me, and we were not starting from scratch as we now trained for the biggest competition in our sport. The simple fact, however, is he was not Coach Kimball. This was the Olympics after all, and I truly wished the coach who trained me to be an Olympian would be with me at the Mexico Olympics.

I tried to let it go and focused on Coach Billingsley's help and guidance. Coach selection for Olympic teams often created frustration and comfort issues among U.S. athletes in all sports. This situation would later become a reason why I became more involved in athlete advocacy.

Now, as the first day of competition in Mexico drew closer, the anticipation about what was ahead grew. I realized I had to stay focused on diving — not on all the fun surrounding the Olympic Village and the Olympians from countries with names I couldn't even pronounce. And, I caught myself wanting to hurry through practice and get back to the excitement in the Village. That's when the surprise I desperately needed happened: I arrived at the pool as usual and there was Coach Kimball standing by the diving board waiting for me!

My parents were able to cover Coach Kimball's expenses to go to Mexico to be there for me. I am forever grateful they managed to make that happen. And yes, it was Coach Billingsley who got Coach Kimball a coach's pass that allowed him on the pool deck. Having Coach Kimball there meant so much to me. I felt so ready going into the competition the next day.

As a "first time" Olympian, the Olympic Village was incredible. I thought all other athletes were like me and only spoke their native language. Being so naïve about the wider world, I think many of us didn't realize that people from other countries, unlike Americans, often must learn multiple languages from birth. The paltry three or four years of Spanish or French that many in my generation were taught in high school would not take us very far abroad.

Those first couple of days, we'd all be yakking away obliviously in English, not realizing that the Italians, Russians, and Germans could understand every word we "English speakers" were saying.

During a practice session, one of the Canadian guy divers turned to a Russian diver and asked in a very friendly tone, "Does your mother wear combat boots?" a common insult at the time. All the girl divers were shocked by this, but he asked again, using that same tone to make it sound like a friendly question rather than the put-down that he intended. The other English-speaking male divers sniggered — they were in on the joke.

The Russian men shot the Canadian and American men some odd looks, but didn't respond. The Canadian and American women divers admonished the guys openly for being such jerks, but the guys didn't listen to us, insisting that the Russians couldn't understand what the Canadian diver had said.

It seemed pretty clear to me that everyone knew they were being jerks whether they understood the exact words or the context, but there was no open confrontation, and we moved on from the incident. I thought little more of it until a couple of days later when the long-awaited Olympic diving prelims finally rolled around.

The day before, I had left my Olympic credential in my locker and could not enter the Village without it, so I went back to the pool to pick it up. I walked into the locker room and sitting there alone was one of the Russian girls.

I gave her a nod and a smile and went to my locker for the credential. I felt like she was staring at me and wanted to engage. So I turned toward her. She looked straight at me and said in perfect English, "Your boy divers were saying mean things to us the other day."

Wow.

My jaw dropped. Clearly, all of us had grossly underestimated the level of English-language proficiency the Soviets had attained. At first, I felt embarrassed, but she understood the dynamic, and that moment was the beginning of an incredibly special Olympic friendship.

Her name was Svetlana. She was a platform diver, which was great, because that meant we wouldn't be diving against each other directly. We talked for almost an hour the day we met; I didn't realize how long we'd been in the locker room yakking like a couple of childhood best friends. Her coach would be furious to know she was meeting secretly with an American.

We had so much in common and so much to talk about, so we arranged to meet in the locker room as often as possible. She felt safe meeting me there, beyond the view of the KGB and her teammates. But we had to be careful, she said. No one on the Russian team could know we were friends. This was not about athletics — it was about the Cold War.

I was dismayed when she revealed this. It hadn't occurred to me the kind of pressures the Soviet athletes were under; I was blissfully unaware of just how high the stakes were for these athletes.

At the time, the Cold War was in full swing, and the Soviets were waging a battle against the capitalist West. This meant their athletes came under intense pressure at any international competition. If they didn't win, that somehow cast shame on the Soviet Union.

In response to any loss or failure to attain established goals, the athletes would face admonishment from their government, their coaches, and their countrymen. They were sent home immediately if they lost. Rumor had it they sometimes ended up in a Siberian gulag for disgracing the Soviet Union.

That heavy weight of expectation — to be on the podium and bring glory to the Mother Land — was a dreadful position for these athletes to be in, and it made the Olympics a very fraught experience for them. That's before we even talk about how these athletes were being followed everywhere they went by KGB operatives who were there to prevent them from defecting to the West.

So, with a vague understanding of this context, I found Svetlana quietly crying in the locker room a day later.

"What's wrong?" I asked.

She shrugged. "I need to win a medal or they will send me home in disgrace," she said. Her lips trembled as she spoke.

This brought home to me just how high the stakes were for her; if she didn't perform well, who knew what might happen to her and her family?

I sat down beside her and put my hand on her shoulder. "You can't do anything but your best," I said.

It felt weak, but I had no idea what else to say at that moment. I know my American platitudes couldn't soothe her, but a hug and my sincere empathy seemed the best I could do to show I was her friend. I did not doubt she would dive well.

As I stood up to head back to the pool, she smiled and said, "I love how you do your back 1½." Yes. She had become a special friend.

The next day, Svetlana competed in the platform event and did not medal. True to her prediction, she was immediately sent home. I never saw her again.

Some 30 years later, I was at a meet in Fort Lauderdale.

Divers had come from all over the world, including Australia, Europe, and Russia. It's a huge competition that we look forward to every year. I was there as a judge, enjoying the Florida sunshine. The last day of the meet, as we were wrapping up proceedings and I was gathering my things together, a young man came up to me. He asked if I was Micki King.

"Yes, I'm Micki King. Who are you?"

"I'm Svetlana's son. She asked me to give you a hug for the friendship you showed her," he said in perfect English as he enveloped me in his arms.

I was speechless. What an incredible surprise. He told me that although his mother hadn't won a medal in the Olympics, life worked out alright for her in the end. Her son carried on the diving tradition, and it was his solemn duty to find me and tell me how big an impact my friendship made on his mother.

I'll forever remember Svetlana as a great example of just how powerful sports can be to overcome the politics that would otherwise keep us apart.

✶ ✶ ✶

Making new international friendships was special, but I was in Mexico City to win, and I directed all my energy to getting the job done. As an Air Force lieutenant at the time, I had the added weight of representing America's armed forces in the competition. And that added to my motivation for gold.

I knew I was capable of it, but there's always that element of luck in any sporting event. I just had to keep my head in the game and dive like I knew I could.

For the vast majority of the competition, that's exactly what I did. And heading into that 9th of 10 dives in the finals of the women's 3-meter springboard, I felt I had turned in a podium-worthy performance.

But then I hit the board. I stumbled. I missed the mark, and that threw the door open wide to the other women who were trying just as hard as I was to make Olympic history.

My teammate Sue Gossick walked right through that door I opened, answering my flub with a superlative dive of her own.

Heading into my last dive, I knew I had to pull off something miraculous if I wanted to claim a podium spot. Gold seemed out of the question. Yet, I still had a shot at silver or bronze if I could stay focused.

Yes, my arm hurt. In fact, it throbbed. But the show must go on, right? So I pulled myself together to shake off the pain. Big girls don't cry, and here I was on the world stage. It was time to put up or shut up.

The good news was, this last dive was my breadwinner dive — a reverse 1½ somersault with 1½ twists. I had put it last because it was my signature dive, and not many women were doing this dive at the time.

I was known for this dive — I owned it. I knew if I nailed it, I could still climb the podium. Easy, right?

Coach Kimball pulled me aside to give me a pep talk as my turn to dive approached. He put a hand on my shoulder and said earnestly, "This is the biggest dive of your life. You've done it a million times. Just concentrate on your hurdle."

I nodded. That sounded easy enough.

"You're leaning back on the end of the board," he said. "Adjust it so that your weight is straight up and down," he said, pulling his spine straight and making himself as tall as he could.

I nodded again. Yes. Coach Kimball was right, and I understood how to fix it. I took a deep breath as the loudspeaker blared my name and announced my dive. My dive. My dive. I could do this. I climbed the ladder to the board for my final dive at the Mexico Olympic Games.

I stood for a moment longer than usual at the back of the board, running through one last visualization of the dive. I took a steadying breath and began.

I nailed the hurdle just as we'd discussed, and for an instant, I felt overwhelming relief. I was going to do this. But then a nanosecond later, nerve-searing pain shot through me. As I wrapped my arms around my torso to execute the twist, I jostled the injury from the dive before and the pain in my arm utterly overtook me. I wasn't ready for the pain! It caught me completely off guard. I did a "spaghetti dive" — I completely fell apart.

You can see it on film taken at the meet. I start off well, and then in mid-air, I collapse and my dive disintegrates. For the second time in that competition, I sank into the pool and thought about disappearing down the drain.

When I surfaced, I saw 2s and 3s on the judges' scorecards. It was over. There was nothing I could do. It was my final dive that cost me the medal at the 1968 Games, not the dive when I hit the board. Before I'd struggled out of the water, I knew beyond any shadow of a doubt that I would not be taking home any hardware. My Olympic experience had amounted to little more than an incredibly painful arm and a lot of heartache.

Looking back now, I wish Coach Kimball had simply told me to be ready for the arm pain when I did my last dive. Granted, none of us knew at that moment that I had actually broken my arm. That revelation came hours later, well after I had finished in fourth place with no podium climb. I painfully got dressed and went to see the medical staff on site.

They took an X-ray of my arm and found I fractured it when I hit the board on dive nine. No wonder it hurt! The medical staff were sympathetic and impressed that I'd managed to finish the competition, given the severity of the injury. They put me in a cast, and I left the doctor feeling even more glum with this awful, unwieldy souvenir of a Games gone wrong. I'd be arriving back home from Mexico with a cast on my arm instead of a medal around my neck.

But then, as I walked slowly back towards the Village feeling sorry for myself, a funny thing happened. Several athletes stopped me to express their sympathies. They knew my name. They praised my diving. They wanted to shake my hand. They wanted to sign my cast.

As disappointed as I was about not medaling, I soon realized there was a big perk to how it all ended up. Word got around quickly and everyone had something nice to say to me. I had become the belle of the ball not because I'd won, but because I'd persevered.

I never imagined that I might become a storyline of the Olympic Games. I had hoped my tale would be one of singular triumph, but I soon realized I couldn't do anything about what had happened. The attention and compassion I received from so many athletes — especially the good-looking guys — made me realize there was an opportunity here to make the best of a less-than-ideal situation. I may not have won, but I was still the fourth best diver in the world that day.

I decided to just have fun with it. Everyone wanted to sign my cast, so I sure let them. It was a great icebreaker, and I managed to meet and talk to just about every athlete in the Olympic Village, it seemed. Before long, I had collected so many signatures on my cast, there wasn't any room left.

As it turned out, I had one of the most amazing Olympic experiences one can have; though my event didn't turn out the way I wanted, I went home having met athletes from literally every corner of the globe. I wasn't going home with a medal, but

Interview with Keith Jackson

I was going home with so many wonderful memories — of friends won, experiences had, and a new perspective gained.

My cast is a unique piece of Olympic history, covered with the signatures of athletes from all over the world. Its permanent home is at the International Swimming Hall of Fame in Fort Lauderdale, and it will remain there in perpetuity as a testament to the true spirit of the Games.

All because of diving.

CHAPTER 5

UNSLIPPING THE FALL

"People, even more than things, have to be restored, renewed, revived, reclaimed, and redeemed; never throw out anyone."

—Audrey Hepburn, British actress and humanitarian

Living with the mistake that cost me that medal was hard, but I grew from that experience. I learned about the true spirit of the Olympic Games in the conversations I had with folks wanting to sign my cast, and the slew of new friends I made along the way.

But living with that failure weighed on me, especially because I truly believed my diving career was over. I'd done my best at the Olympics Games, and it didn't work out. That's how the cookie crumbles sometimes, I figured.

At the time, it was unusual for an athlete to compete in more than one Games — the quadrennial cycle made it very difficult for athletes to stay in the mix long-term, especially because amateur status was everything back then; we didn't have sponsors. We were totally amateurs on every front. My sponsor was my Mom and Dad, covering all my expenses until I was in the Air Force and could support myself. And then, the Air Force was the huge difference maker.

That's just how it was back then. Olympic athletes didn't make any money from their sport, and being able to train at that level and support oneself wasn't easy and not something most athletes could sustain for more than one quadrennial. The Olympics were a once-in-a-lifetime opportunity, and I'd had mine.

Instead of crying over spilled milk, I did my best to let it go. Sure, I still thought about it with a tinge of regret, but it was time to shift into the next stage of my life. It was time to focus on my Air Force career, to complete my service, and move on with my life. And that meant moving 2,000 miles west to Los Angeles, where the Air Force reassigned me in the summer of 1969.

I packed up what I could fit in my car and left Michigan for California. Yes, it was scary to leave Michigan. My parents, my sister, my cousins, my life as I'd known it for 24 years was there. I watched it slip away in my rear-view mirror as I drove off.

Luckily, I quickly found a fabulous little apartment in Hermosa Beach, right on the Pacific Ocean. I could see the waves from my window, rather a novelty for a Michigan girl who'd grown up in the landlocked center of America.

I really enjoyed living in the Los Angeles area. I was young, and I quickly settled in. Before I knew it, I realized I was at peace without diving. I was happy to be contributing as an Air Force officer working 8 to 5 in an office at the Los Angeles Air Force Station (now called Los Angeles Air Force Base), pulling my weight and soon to be moving up in the ranks. This was how my life was supposed to go; fate had set the arc of my story, and I gamely followed. It was all good.

But then something unexpected happened: the National AAU Championships were held at the Belmont Pool in Long Beach, California in April 1969 — the same pool where I'd qualified for the Olympics in 1968 — about a 20-minute drive from my L.A. apartment. (Today, that same journey would probably take upwards of an hour, but in the late 1960s, L.A. traffic wasn't what it is today.)

I couldn't wait to watch those Nationals. And when I got there, I knew everyone on the pool deck. I was immediately swept up in a string of fierce hugs and joyful welcomes as we swapped stories and warm memories. Then I headed to the bleachers to watch the meet.

There I was, just watching when I realized, I shouldn't be in the bleachers. I should be in line for my turn to dive. I'd left the sport behind, and I missed it intensely.

I wasn't prepared for that feeling. After the meet, I spoke with Glenn McCormick, the legendary coach at the Belmont pool, and asked him if I could join his team.

"Are you kidding me?" he asked, incredulous.

I wasn't expecting that response.

"No," I stammered. "I was just hoping maybe I could come dive with you and your team sometime?"

He laughed. "Of course you can dive with us! We'd love to have you join us."

And so, a few days later, I started attending workouts at the Belmont pool. With the vitality of youth on my side, I slipped seamlessly back into my skill set. I hadn't lost much fitness, despite having spent 108 days in a bulky, cumbersome arm cast. The smooth, graceful movements I'd trained for so long were still there, tucked deep in my muscle memory.

My diving reflex triggered, it took but a few heartbeats to reestablish my diving rhythm and routine. I thoroughly enjoyed playing at diving that summer and hanging out with divers again. I was happy to be working with Coach McCormick, who had guided a generous handful of Olympians over the years. He was a great guy and certainly knew his way around a diving board. In June 1969, the Air Force Sports Program, of course, took me back, and that year, I took part in an International Military Sports Council championship in Pescara, Italy. There, I competed against men but still managed to finish fourth in the springboard and third in the platform. It all began to fall into place.

I was back.

Before I knew it, the 1972 Olympic Trials loomed on the horizon. I felt confident that I was back in shape again and stood a good chance of qualifying for a second Olympic team.

The Air Force wholly supported my Olympic quest, and I attended Trials at the Oakton Pool in Park Ridge, a suburb of Chicago, at the end of July.

The Trials were just another meet for me. Now, diving was all business — it wasn't a hobby and it wasn't like I was new to this. I was a veteran of this Olympic thing and I wanted to be the one to beat. The press dubbed me "Mother Maxine" because I was much older than the other competitors — I had 11 years on Ulrika Knape of Sweden and 10 years on American diver Janet Ely.

While 28 was considered "old" to still be competitive, I carried that fact comfortably and gladly. I wasn't going to let gold slip away this time. I went in clear-headed, ready, and calm. This would be my second and for certain last try at Olympic gold. I was focused and mentally ready. Elite performance under pressure is about getting your head right. I knew I was in the right mental space now to excel.

I finished second in the 1972 Olympic Trials. I was 6 points out of first place, behind Cynthia Potter, and well ahead of the third-place diver, Janet Ely. I'd done my job, just like any other day at the office. I was comfortable with my performance and very ready to get to Munich. I realized my mentality was completely different from where I had been four years earlier heading to Mexico.

What was interesting about the 1972 Trials was the number of divers who qualified to represent the United States in Munich. Typically, 12 divers are selected at the Olympic Trials to represent the United States — three men and three women in the springboard event and three men and three women in the 10-meter platform event. But the 1972 Trials produced only eight divers from the U.S. Only three women in total would represent the United States: Cynthia Potter, then 21, of Houston; Janet Ely, just 18 years, old from Albuquerque; and me, at the ripe old age of 28. We were the first group of female divers since 1948 to "double" by each qualifying in both the platform and the springboard events, and our success showed our versatility and depth. On the men's side, one man, Michael Finneran, doubled, so only five men were headed to Munich instead of the usual six.

After the Trials, Hobie Billingsley was announced to be the team coach again, and he told *Swimming World* magazine that "We may be small, but this is the toughest all-around diving squad we've ever had." The only problem was, as Coach Billingsley noted, "Both our guys and gals are going to face about the toughest foreign competition ever. But we are ready for them, and we won't give an inch."

✶ ✶ ✶

What I didn't know at the time but learned some years later, was that my return to diving and my eventual ascension to the 1972 U.S. Olympic Team wasn't quite as serendipitous or as self-directed as I thought.

You know how in some television shows, the clever protagonist always seems to know exactly how the other characters are going to react in a certain situation and they've already strategized four moves ahead to get that person into the exact place they want? Well, that's what was happening around me in 1968 and 1969.

What had seemed like mere fate, I learned, was really the work of larger forces, namely the will of my coach, Dick Kimball. After the 1968 Olympics, Coach Kimball had gotten on the phone to the Air Force Sports Office in San Antonio, where Air Force athlete duties and assignments were managed, and told them, "She's not done yet. She can't let this go. She's got more in this, and Olympic gold is still possible."

The Air Force agreed, and that's how I ended up in Los Angeles and in Glenn McCormick's orbit. Kimball had arranged with Glenn to coach me with his team and had set it all up. It was rigged from the outset; Kimball knew I wasn't finished. All he needed to do was make a few phone calls, and it was organized.

They knew more about me than I knew about me at the time.

Coach Kimball, our perspicacious protagonist, knew for sure that I would watch the AAU Nationals at the Belmont pool that summer of 1969. And he intuited what would happen the minute I stepped into the Long Beach pool. I played right into his hands. Dick Kimball knew me better than I knew myself.

There's more than one way to skin a cat, so to speak, and as it turns out, there's more than one way to lure a consummate diver back to her perch without her realizing what's happening. I was 100% all-in once again, and this time, I crossed my fingers that I would not come home with a broken bone and a cast full of great stories. I wanted to return with gold around my neck.

All because of diving.

CHAPTER 6

MUNICH

"Pressure makes diamonds."

**— George S. Patton Jr., U.S. Army General
during World War II**

When I arrived in Munich, I had a very different mindset from where I'd been four years earlier heading to Mexico. I was not that star-stuck, somewhat naïve, 24-year-old "hoping" to do well — and who had never traveled much beyond Michigan before. No, I was over all of that. I'd grown up. I'd been diving for more than 10 years and already been to one Olympics. I was all business now.

While the Olympics were bigger and way more exciting than Nationals — the television cameras dotted around the pool deck made that clear if it wasn't already achingly obvious — in the end it didn't change anything. Winning was winning, and I knew I had to take everything, including the surroundings and the competition, in stride. I now had the experience that breeds confidence in pressure-cooker situations. And I trusted myself. What's more, I was aided by a mission — to win the gold that eluded me in Mexico.

It was time to soar.

* * *

The 1972 Olympic Games began on August 26th and the diving events kicked off the very next day, starting with the preliminary round of the women's 3-meter springboard.

This timeline suited me: I had unfinished business to attend to, and the sooner we could get going, the better.

Of course, none of the other divers felt bad about what happened to me in Mexico City; none of them felt the gold in Munich was my medal to win. They all wanted that medal for their own. I knew I needed to perform my very best to defend my media-anointed position as "the one to beat."

Despite this pressure, I was ready when I stepped on the board for the first of my seven dives in the preliminary round. I needed to be in the top 12 to advance to finals. But my score in the prelims carried a lot of weight as it would be added to my final score. In the final round, each diver performs three voluntary dives that have no degree-of-difficulty limit. Final ranking was calculated on the combined score from both days. So, if I blew it during prelims, I'd be digging myself a hole with only three dives left to increase my lead — and win!

Despite that pressure, I dived well during the prelim. Really, in many respects, it was just another day at the office, but it wasn't a perfect showing. I scored 289.14 points and moved on to finals in third place.

Knowing that the scores from prelims would count toward my total, I worried that my prelim score might not be good enough for gold. But my three voluntary dives were high-scorers, and I was less than three points behind Ulrika Knape, the Swedish phenom, who had won that first round. Still, I was uneasy; I expected I would be first at the end of prelims, and being in third gave me a moment's pause. Had I done enough in that first round to ensure success in the second?

This is when Coach Kimball pulled me aside and gave me perhaps the second greatest gift he could as a coach.

"It's OK that you're a few points behind," he said.

Say what? I stared at him, confused. I don't think I'd ever heard Coach Kimball say it was OK to be behind in the standings. Ever.

"What are you talking about?" I asked.

He shook his head. "I'm serious. You're in the perfect position," he said. "It's just a couple of points and you can make those up in the finals."

I wasn't convinced and gave him that look I did whenever I didn't catch his drift.

"Coach, did you just give me permission to be behind?" I asked, incredulous.

He nodded. "Yes. Just go back to your room and forget about the prelims."

I was just three-and-a-half points out of first place, so I suppose he had a point.

"Coach, I'm not sure I get it," I pressed. "We've been together for 10 years and this is the first time you've said it's OK to be behind. Why is that?"

He pointed across the pool to where the two Swedish divers who were in first and second place were surrounded by reporters. They must have had four microphones in their faces and a couple of television cameras zooming in on them. There was no way they were getting off that pool deck anytime soon. The Olympic television broadcast had become a very hot commodity, and the media had airwaves to pack with content. Obtaining a pool-side interview with the cute, young, blonde gals who were leading the first diving event of the Games was a real "get" for those reporters.

"We don't need that," Coach Kimball said.

Suddenly, I understood what Coach Kimball was trying to tell me. The pressure was off me and now on Ulrika Knape and her teammate Agneta Henriksson.

He "gave me permission" to be behind, go back to my room, and get myself ready for the finals. He was right. I didn't need that attention, and I seized the opportunity for what it was — a chance to chill out beyond the glare of the press so I could shine my brightest in finals. I headed back to my room in the Olympic Village to prepare for my last three dives at the Olympic Games in Munich.

When it was time to go back to the pool, I carefully packed my bag. I folded and refolded my lucky towel before tucking it in alongside my other gear. Any athlete who doesn't admit to being superstitious and having lucky talismans they bring to every major competition is lying. We all do it, and I fully embraced the ritual of packing my bag while thinking about the dives to come.

I guess I was feeling especially superstitious as I picked up my official Team USA sweatpants and jacket. I looked at them for a long moment, feeling their warm weight in my hand. You're required to wear this uniform on the podium if you win a medal, so the most logical thing I could do was to pack it in my Team USA bag and lug it to the pool. I'm sure every other member of

Team USA had their USA sweats in their bag, in hopes they'd be on the podium.

But, I was suddenly seized with the concern that if I brought my USA podium gear to the pool — I might not need it. Ouch, I thought. I really wanted to need my USA warm-ups, so, in an effort to not jinx myself, I purposely left my Team USA warm-up gear folded neatly on my bed in the Olympic Village.

When I got to the pool, Coach Kimball was already there. He patted me on the back and assured me, "You've got this." And I knew he was right. I knew I had this in a way I'd never felt before. Down to my bones — including the one I'd broken in Mexico — I knew I could succeed. So, I just got on with it.

I had three dives left, and they were my bread and butter, high-point dives.

I executed those dives cleanly, with perfection and as much grace as I had ever mustered before. It was so different from my experience in Mexico City; there was no stabbing pain or regretful resurfacing after a botched dive. In Munich, I nailed every one of those dives. And I knew it.

After my last dive, I popped up and saw Coach Kimball standing at the side of the pool looking toward the judges. In another instance of adrenaline-fueled math prowess, his posture changed the instant the judges flipped their cards. He knew I'd won and let out a shout and waved his arms above his head. I'd just become an Olympic champion. My dream had come true. Finally.

To say I felt relief would be an understatement, but I also felt immense gratitude for everything that brought me to this moment. And I felt vindicated. To come back and win Olympic gold at age 28, well, that meant something. Having failed in 1968 only added to the sense of accomplishment I felt in 1972. All the sacrifice, all the hard work, was so worth it. It was a complicated set of emotions to process.

Immediately after that final dive, an event staffer approached me as I was toweling off and said, "It's time to be at the podium." The television cameras were rolling, and they were ready to start the medal ceremony. "We can't hold up the TV, get your sweats on now."

I was in real trouble. Yeah. I needed my podium gear, as I'd hoped, but it was back in the dorm. Uh-oh.

I looked around and saw Janet Ely standing off to the side. Janet, my Michigan teammate from the "no girls in the men's pool" days was my Olympic teammate, too. She had finished in fourth place so would not be on the podium. She was wearing her warm-up pants.

I rushed over. "Janet! I've gotta go, they're calling me, but I left my USA warm-up pants in my room. I need to wear them on the podium. Can I borrow yours?" I asked.

"Oh, yeah! Sure! Of course!" she said, with a big smile. It didn't occur to me until after the fact that it might have been slightly insensitive to ask the fourth-place finisher if her warm-up pants could climb the podium without her in them. But in this moment of panic, I had to ask. Janet was as gracious as could be — she stripped her warm-up pants off right there and handed them to me.

So now I needed a USA team jacket. Again, I looked around the pool, and on the other side of the deck, I saw a guy from the boxing team wearing a pair of jeans and his Team USA jacket. I knew his name was James Busceme and he went by Bubba. He had snuck onto the pool deck for a closer view of the diving competition.

I marched right over to him and said, "Hey, Bubba! I need your swag! I don't have mine with me, and they're calling me for the medal presentation. Can I borrow your USA jacket?"

He stared at me for a second and said, "You mean my jacket will be part of an Olympic podium ceremony?"

I nodded.

He couldn't get it unzipped fast enough. He handed it to me and I ran toward the podium, zipping in as I went, shouting, "Thanks, Bubba!" over my shoulder.

Finally, I was ready. I'd been rescued by my amazing Team USA friends. Panting from the race around the pool, I got in line to step on the podium in the right order: third, first, second. And, yes, I felt complete relief as we started the walk to the winner's podium. It had all worked out!

I was finally relaxed. I let out a big breath and casually put my hand in Bubba's pocket, where I found something squishy. I pulled my hand out, now covered with melted chocolate. Yuck!

Turned out, the heat inside the natatorium had melted a chocolate bar Bubba had saved in his jacket pocket for later. Yuck again! Another instant of panic, but all I could do was wipe the chocolate off — onto Janet's pants. What's more, she's a good five inches shorter than me, so as I climbed onto the Olympic podium, it became embarrassingly obvious that I was wearing highwater pants to accept my precious gold medal. But at least I was in an official uniform — even if the legs were too short and the jacket too big.

People often ask me what emotions I felt as I stood atop the Olympic podium to receive my gold medal. Truth be told, I was totally freaked out as I stood there receiving my Olympic gold medal while wiping Bubba's melted chocolate bar all over Janet's Olympic warm-ups, there wasn't room for much else.

✷ ✷ ✷

But there's more. After the medal ceremony, we three medalists were whisked away for a urinalysis to check for doping violations. Olympic organizers take that procedure very seriously, and I couldn't even return the clothes I'd borrowed to Janet and Bubba. The staffers told me they couldn't let me out of their sight until I'd peed in the cup. They had to be sure I wasn't cheating on the test.

At the same time, the USA divers and my Olympic buddies were headed to the Hofbräuhaus, a huge and very famous beer hall in central Munich. Of course I wanted to go with them immediately, but peeing in a cup came first. I told them, "Save me a seat, I'll catch up after I'm done here."

We followed the officials down to a waiting area for the test. Of course, Ulrika Knape and Marina Janicke, who I'd just beaten on the most prestigious stage in the sport, were no happier than I was to be sitting there. But none of us could leave. So, we sat there drinking water — lots of water!

The wait was endless; I had probably peed 20 times before the finals because of nerves, and now, I couldn't pee at all. So, I sat there with them drinking glass after glass of water.

Finally, Ulrika broke the silence by saying, "Did you see that the medals have our names on them?" She held hers up and pointed to the thin edge where tiny block letters spelled out her name, perfect in its precision and clarity.

I flipped mine over and squinted. Sure enough, there was my name, on my medal too, plain as day, spelled out in small letters:

King | Nicki

Yikes!

The priceless medal I'd just won an hour earlier had my name spelled wrong! I couldn't believe it. How did they mess that up? Seriously.

"Huh, they have my name wrong," I said ruefully, holding out the edge for the other two divers to see.

"Oh, no! That's horrible!" they said.

Then, Marina said, "I think the engraver is still here. Maybe he can fix it for you?"

Yes, yes, yes! Excellent idea. After I finally produced the urine sample, I trekked off to the bowels of the natatorium to find the engraver.

After some searching, I found the room where the medals were being engraved and banged on the door. A big, burly German man stuck his head out.

"Vas do you vant?" he asked. *Oh, dear,* I thought. The language barrier.

I took a deep breath, and slowly said, "My name is Micki. M-I-C-K-I. But my medal says Nicki. N-I-C-K-I. Can you fix?" I asked slowly, while pointing to the misspelled name.

He rolled his eyes and grabbed the medal, muttering something I didn't understand. He disappeared back into the room, slamming the door behind him.

I could hear him talking to someone else in rapid-fire German, sounding very annoyed, of course, but I didn't understand a word.

Finally, he reappeared. Holding the medal out to me, he said in broken English, "We decide, much easier to change your name than to change medal."

✳ ✳ ✳

I never did make it to the Hofbräuhaus that night. By the time I'd completed my drug test, talked with the engraver, and finally got back into my own clothes, three hours had gone by and the celebratory moment had passed. I just wasn't in the mood anymore.

It was past midnight when I finally left the pool and the cool air hit me smack in the face; with a dark sky overhead and stillness all around, I didn't feel much like yakking and yelling and whooping it up. I was also hungry, so I headed to the cafeteria, which mercifully was open 24 hours a day for the hordes of voracious athletes.

At that late hour, however, this liminal space was completely devoid of other athletes. The silence soothed me, and it was a perfect time to be by myself.

I walked up to the counter where a few sleepy workers were manning the food stations. "I want the biggest ice cream sundae you can make me," I told one of them.

He smiled and pointed to the sundae bar. "You can make your own."

I marched over and proceeded to make myself the most enormous sundae I've ever seen. I took that bad boy over to a table in the huge, empty dining hall and sat quietly by myself devouring it. I couldn't believe how good it tasted — a sweet, sweet reward if ever there were one.

A few moments later, the doors at the back of the cafeteria flew open and three noisy men walked in, laughing and talking excitedly. I wasn't keen on being interrupted, and I did my best to ignore them. I tried to give off that vibe that says, "I just want to be by myself."

Apparently, that subtle communication didn't work — one of them noticed me straight away and said loudly to the others, "Over there! She's American! Let's go sit with her!" They made a beeline for me carrying trays laden with food.

It turned out they were Australian weightlifters. They had all this gear, and for just three guys, they made a lot of noise as they settled in around me, eradicating my tranquil repast.

"We just finished our match and our friend here, he just got fourth," one of them told me with so much exuberance, I couldn't help but grin. "We're so proud of him and we just want to celebrate!" He paused to take a bite.

"How about you? How'd you do?" another asked.

It was at that moment that all three of them noticed "the box." It was just sitting there, next to my tray, but it was one of those boxes that every athlete at the Games coveted. Everyone knew it contained a medal, and there were scant few of these boxes to go around. A hush descended over them.

"Is that?..." one companion asked, pointing at the box.

"Can we see it?" another one asked.

I nodded and pushed the box toward the middle of the table. One of them reached out and lifted the lid, revealing that it wasn't just any medal, it was gold. I think one of them gasped, but then, it got so quiet, you could hear a heartbeat. Silently, each one of them stood and bowed toward me. Their reverence was beyond flattering, and I thought, "Wow, this is really cool."

I was overcome with a warm feeling of the spirit of the Olympic Games. Here were these handsome guys who I didn't know and who didn't know the first thing about me, but who understood exactly what went into claiming that box with the medal. I suddenly felt like celebrating again.

Their moment of veneration completed, one of them shouted, "Yippee! A gold medal! We will celebrate with you!"

Another one pulled out a bottle of wine he had spirited into the cafeteria under his jacket, and then we were all toasting my Olympic medal and having a party.

And that's how I celebrated my Olympic gold medal in Munich, with three guys I didn't know, from literally the other side of the planet. And you know what? It was absolutely marvelous. It was exactly what I needed and so poignantly perfect to have that moment with those Olympians. The Hofbräuhaus would not have equaled this.

Somehow, they knew just how to make my day even better than it already was and helped me process the momentous feat I'd accomplished a few hours prior. I finally, truly, embraced the idea that I had achieved my goal.

I had become an Olympic champion.

✶ ✶ ✶

I was so excited about having won gold in the springboard that the 10-meter platform event, for which I had also qualified, had become almost an afterthought. But I still had one more event to compete in at the Munich Games, and it was my duty to turn in the best performance I could.

Each diver completed five dives on September 1st and as with the springboard competition, the top 12 advanced to the finals. Again, I passed through easily in fifth place. I was about 20 points back from Milena Duchková, the Czechoslovakian diver who had finished in first place during the preliminary round with 225.00 points, but I was less than a point behind the third-place diver, Marina Janicke of East Germany, who had scored 206.73 in the prelim. Another medal wasn't out of the question.

During the final the next day, we 12 divers performed three voluntary dives each, and the final ranking was based on the combined score with the preliminary round. I added another 141.30 points to the 205.08 I'd scored the day before, bringing me to a grand total of 346.38 points. That left me solidly in fifth place; I ended up a little over 14 points behind Janicke, who claimed the bronze medal. My fellow American, Janet Ely, finished in fourth place again, just 8 points back from Janicke. It wasn't to be for the American women in the platform event.

Nevertheless, I was thrilled with the shiny gold medal I had collected — even if my name was misspelled. I soon came to embrace that piece of the story, too. One letter engraved incorrectly couldn't begin to negate the fact that I'd earned that medal through so many years of hard work, dedication, and a lot of good fortune.

After my events wrapped up, I now had free time to enjoy the whole Olympic experience. I stayed in the athlete's village and attended every competition I could get into. I was still knocking around the campus on September 5th when the terrorist attacks occurred.

It was an especially cruel way for politics to crush our otherwise safe and sport-focused reverie. It started before sunrise on September 5th, when eight members of the Palestinian extremist group Black September scaled an unguarded fence surrounding the Olympic Village and infiltrated the dorm where the Israeli delegation slept.

Back then, we came and went freely from the village with virtually no security checks. In fact, my sister used my athlete badge to gain entrance into the village a few times, that's how loose security was. Prior to the attack, there was little reason to think anyone could come to harm inside the athlete's village, but that innocence evaporated when those terrorists burst into the building where the Israeli team was staying.

American housing was parallel to the Israeli quarters, but even with being so close to the tragedy, it took hours for an official to tell us what was happening. The only news source was German radio — which we could not understand. We could see commotion, but we didn't have any details for a long time. We just knew something terrible had transpired.

Eventually, information reached us about the terrorist attack that killed two members of the Israeli team. A hostage situation ensued when the terrorists held nine other Israeli athletes and coaches while they tried to bargain for the release of Palestinian prisoners in Israel. Eventually, we learned that all of the hostages, five of their captors, and a policeman had been killed in a botched rescue attempt undertaken by West German authorities.

Soon thereafter, we learned that Olympic officials had decided to cancel the rest of the Olympic Games because of this terrible turn of events. It was an understandable impulse, but it was the wrong answer. Cancelling the rest of the Munich Olympics would be a "win" for the Palestinian terrorists.

It didn't take long for the 1972 Olympic athletes from every country to push back on the officials and convince them that cancelling the rest of the Games was not the right choice. This uproar from the athletes in Munich was resounding and the officials were forced to reconsider. The decision was made to pause the Games for a day of mourning to recognize the loss of the Israeli athletes and coaches. The Games then commenced the following day.

While Avery Brundage, still the head of the IOC at the time, received a lot of criticism for the decision to continue the Games after the attacks, I felt it was the correct call, and I am so proud of the world athletes who helped make that happen. We managed to pull together and force "the Suits" (as we called the Olympic officials who made all the decisions about and for the athletes but never asked for athlete input) to not ignore us any longer.

This experience in Munich left a huge impression on me. And before long, I would become more involved in bringing athletes' needs and rights into the light. But at that moment, it was time to head home and lean into my Air Force career.

CHAPTER 7

CELEBRITY STATUS

*"I'm more interested in being
good than being famous."*

— **Annie Leibovitz, American portrait photographer**

Winning a gold medal changes your life, but not always in the ways you might expect. One of the least expected was helping Johnny Carson perform a challenging diving stunt on national television.

A month after I got back from Munich, I was invited onto *The Tonight Show Starring Johnny Carson* with Coach Kimball. Johnny was known for doing crazy things on his show. So Coach Kimball suggested they set up a trampoline and spotting rig the day we were guests.

The comedian hammed it up for the crowd, and in short order, with Coach Kimball guiding, Johnny Carson did a near perfect back somersault on the stage to thunderous applause from the studio audience — along with everyone watching at home, I'm sure.

It was great to meet Johnny and have the whole late-night TV experience — it was a real, "Is this actually happening?" kind of moment.

* * *

I don't think it's overstating it to say that if I hadn't been in the Air Force, I would not have competed in the 1972 Olympic Games. But again, as after the 1968 Olympics, I figured I was finished with diving and it was my turn to give back. I readied myself for my next assignment — I was slated for duty at a base in Southeast Asia.

But yet again, external forces intervened.

Shortly after the 1972 Olympic Games, I received a summons from Brigadier General Jeanne Holm to come to Washington, D.C., to meet with her. General Holm was the first female one-star general in the U.S. Air Force and when promoted again, she became the first female two-star general in any military service branch. I couldn't believe she asked to meet me! I assumed the invitation was to congratulate me in person about my gold medal. I was very excited and honored to meet an Air Force general — who also happened to be a woman.

Of course, I took extra care to make sure my uniform was pressed and I was as tidy as possible before heading to General Holm's office. I carried the box with my gold medal in it, ready for her inspection (and maybe she'd even try it on!).

General Holm greeted me with a smile and put me at ease immediately. We talked about Munich, of course, and my family and winters in Michigan. Then suddenly, she got down to business.

"I understand you have orders," she said.

"Yes, ma'am," I replied. "I have orders for Southeast Asia." I explained it was my turn to be deployed now that the Olympics were over.

She smiled and nodded, "I understand you have orders. But you are a female Air Force officer who just won an Olympic gold medal. You need to go somewhere that's notable, and you need to be recognized instead of heading to a remote assignment in the war zone!"

She paused for a moment before asking, "So, what stateside base do you want instead?"

I was stunned. Being asked where I wanted my next duty assignment to be was the very last thing I expected.

"I want to go where I can be most useful," I stammered. "I'm ready to go overseas. I'm ready to take on any duty I'm given. My medal is special, but it's behind me, and I'm ready to move forward."

She shook her head. "You're not hearing me. I want you somewhere in the United States where you can be recognized."

Wow! I sat back in amazement. I had my orders, and I was ready to go...

I sat quietly for another moment, stalling for time. I had no idea what she wanted me to say, since consideration of my preference was something I never expected. I was stumped.

Then suddenly an idea hit.

"The only other Air Force duty that stands out to me is the Air Force Academy," I said. "We trained there before going to Mexico City, and it's a great place."

The athletic facilities at the Academy were top notch, and I could see myself enjoying life at the foot of the Rocky Mountains.

"Hmmm," she said, sitting back in her chair. "The Air Force Academy is an all-male institution."

I nodded and shrugged, expecting her to say this idea would never work. I continued thinking about other places I might be able to suggest.

Instead, she broke into a broad smile. "It's perfect. You'll be the first woman appointed to work at the Air Force Academy, and who better to fill that role than Olympic gold medalist Micki King? It's absolutely perfect."

I wasn't sure what I'd just set in motion, so I tried to protest. But General Holm stopped me. "We can do this. Your next duty is going to be in Colorado at the Air Force Academy. You'll be the first. There aren't even women secretaries there," she said

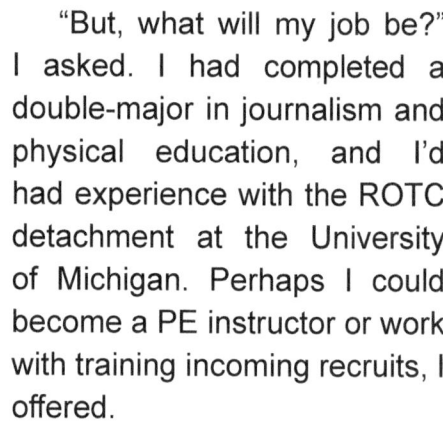

with a sparkle in her eye.

"But, what will my job be?" I asked. I had completed a double-major in journalism and physical education, and I'd had experience with the ROTC detachment at the University of Michigan. Perhaps I could become a PE instructor or work with training incoming recruits, I offered.

General Holm already had an idea. "You'll be the diving coach, of course," she said. "You'll coach the men's team and you'll be on staff as a physical education instructor." She said it with such authority, it felt like the orders had already been printed.

A few days later, I received the formal written orders officially assigning me to the Air Force Academy. It was perfect. It fit my interests and experiences and my undergraduate degree. I couldn't have asked for anything better.

This was just another one of those unexpectedly momentous instances where things fell into place. Just like my first foray into diving when JL LaMont approached me at the pool and talked to me about "flips and somersaults," if General Holm hadn't heard about my success in Munich, if she hadn't thought to invite me to meet with her — there's no way I'd be the person I turned out to be. There was zero reason for her to reach out to me, to go out of her way on my behalf. But I'm so grateful for her insight. (P.S. General Holm did not put the medal on.)

Before I knew it, I was packed and headed to Colorado. I settled in quickly to the new routine, and found that coaching came naturally to me and I loved it.

And that first season, I coached one of my divers, a cadet named Rick McAlister, to a conference championship. That win qualified him for the NCAA Championship meet, and he surprised everyone (except me) when he won! It was the first time a woman had coached a man to an NCAA title.

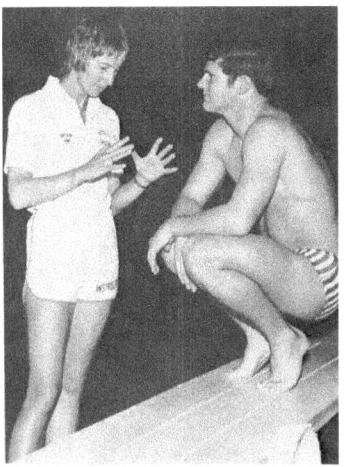

A fun side story is that Barbara McAlister, Rick's sister, was my teammate in Mexico City! Talk about a small world, huh?

Micki with Cadet Rick McAlister.

I also taught tennis and volleyball as a Physical Education instructor during my time at the Academy. I loved my job there, and it meant a lot to open the doors for women at the Academy going forward.

★ ★ ★

The mid-1970s was a landmark time for women. We went from not being able to have our own credit cards in 1972 to suddenly gaining more and more parity with men. Sports was perhaps the most visible aspect of society where these seismic shifts were occurring, and I was lucky to have a circle of friends in women's sports to work alongside to bring more opportunities to girls and women pursuing their athletic dreams. It wasn't easy by a long shot, but as a group, our efforts to create more opportunities for women started the ball rolling.

A remarkable moment in that quest came in 1973 when Bobby Riggs, then 55 years old and long retired from his beloved game of tennis, decided his faded fame needed a little burnishing. Who better to help his "resume" than some of the female tennis stars who were garnering attention for their athletic prowess?

At the height of his career in the late 1930s and 1940s, Riggs had been considered the very best tennis player in the world and was one of the highest paid athletes of the 20th century, reportedly having taken in more than $100,000 over the years — in part because he often placed bets on himself!

Riggs's career was interrupted by naval service during World War II, and by 1973, time had blunted some of the sharper edges of his game. But he was still a hustler and a gambler, and he liked his chances competing against some of the top female players of the era. He asked top-ranked player Billie Jean King to meet him on the court, but she declined, not wanting to be involved in one of his "gimmicks" that could set back the women's liberation or parity in sports movements.

Riggs dangled a $10,000 prize purse as incentive and asked 30-year-old Margaret Court, who was then ranked No. 1. She agreed to the match, which was held on Mother's Day in 1973. Court lost that match, which came to be known as the "Mother's Day Massacre."

Blustering after his victory, Riggs saw dollar signs and a chance to build an even bigger audience. He quickly returned his attention to Billie Jean King, who had made a name for herself as not only a superlative tennis player but also a staunch advocate of women in sports. Riggs played up the male chauvinist ideals behind the contest and made some obnoxious statements, including "Women don't have the emotional stability" to win and that "Women belong in the bedroom and kitchen, in that order." He also called King the "women's libber leader" and said he would beat her whether he had to play her on "clay, grass, wood, cement, marble, or roller skates. We got to keep this sex thing going. I'm a woman specialist now." Whether it was all an act to drum up interest or whether he really believed these things is still up for debate.

Nevertheless, King — who had spent much of 1973 establishing the Women's Tennis Association and threatening to boycott the 1973 U.S. Open if the male and female champions weren't paid the same — took up Riggs's gauntlet. Thanks to rabid public interest in the so-called "Battle of the Sexes," the prize purse ballooned to $100,000. Oddsmakers expected Riggs to win the September 20th match, but King made sure that didn't happen. She played a magnificent game of tennis and properly schooled Riggs on what we women can do. Quite simply, she put him in his place.

When the match was over, Riggs admitted to King that he'd underestimated her.

The televised success of King's dominance of the cocky Riggs — and women's sports in a grander sense — led to additional opportunities for other women athletes. And it began with the widely-acclaimed ABC Sports series called "Women's Superstars."

The program initially started with men, of course. Launched in 1973, the two-hour program called "The Superstars" showcased the athletic talents of 10 men who had achieved some pinnacle of success in a specific sport — think football pros and Olympic athletes — and pitted them against other talented athletes in a variety of tasks designed to showcase each athlete's superior fitness, strength, and agility. The catch was, these consummate athletes couldn't participate in their own sport; for example, an Olympic swimmer wouldn't be able to compete in the swimming competition, but would run a track sprint, play basketball, or volley across the tennis net instead.

It was fascinating to watch these very talented men show their strengths — or well-hidden weaknesses — in sports for which they didn't train. As such, the show became something of a cultural phenomenon. In this scenario, all of these famous athletes were underdogs, and don't we all love an underdog story?

ABC soon decided to capitalize on the social revolution taking place in sports by bringing women into the conversation. In the wake of Billie Jean King's groundbreaking match against Bobby Riggs, the producers of "The Superstars" expanded the franchise to create a women's version, of course. Not alongside the men in the regular "The Superstars" specials, mind you, but in our own program. "Women's Superstars" was slated to hit television screens across the country in January 1975.

I admit I was surprised when the phone rang that day in early 1974 and a producer of the show invited me to take part in the first women's "Superstars" competition. How exciting! Women athletes in 10 different sports would be featured on ABC TV. It was an incredible way to shine a light on women athletes. Finally.

WOMEN'S PRELIMINARY COMPETITION

Linda Jefferson   Micki King   Martina Navratilova

Diana Nyad   Keena Rothhammer   Jackie Tonawanda

AT ROTONDA, JANUARY 19 & 20, 1976

I began training for the competition, working on the sports I was eligible for. The 10 sports we could choose from were tennis, a 350-yard run, basketball, rowing 100 yards, swimming, bowling, a softball throw, a 60-yard dash, a half-mile bike race, and an obstacle course. Luckily, the only one I wasn't "allowed" to do was swimming. (Even though swimming and diving aren't anywhere near the same.)

Thanks to my time in the military, I was adept at land-based sports; all those early-morning ROTC sessions over the years meant I wasn't afraid of a hard run or navigating an obstacle course. And most sports came fairly easily to me. I was cool under pressure and overall quite fit. I really looked forward to meeting these women athletes I'd read about but had never met in person.

It was the first time that so many women of note — there were 12 of us in my preliminary round — from different sports, were in the same place at the same time. It was all thanks to Billie Jean King's unblinking push for equality. Truly, it was a lifetime highlight to be in the mix at the Houston Astrodome for those two days in late December 1974 to film the preliminary rounds of "Women's Superstars."

The prelims aired about a month later and Olympic swimmer Donna de Varona, another pioneer in women's sports and sports broadcasting, served as the announcer. I picked my 7 of 10 sports in that initial outing and finished in first place. What a thrill! A springboard diver winning — on land!

A second prelim round featuring another 12 women took place during the same filming period just before Christmas in 1974. Though I didn't compete with that group directly, I would be facing some of them in the final competition. The top 6 finishers from each group advanced to the finals, which took place in late January 1975. There, I competed against sprinter Wyomia Tyus, skier Kiki Cutter, and gymnast Cathy Rigby along with several other incredible athletes.

In that final round, I amassed a total of 36 points, good for third place overall behind Mary Jo Peppler, an Olympic volleyball player, who'd scored 41 points, and trailblazing basketball player Karen Logan who'd earned 38 points. I knew both of them were tough competitors, so I wasn't shocked by the outcome. And the spectators were very impressed when Mary Jo lobbed a softball so far, it actually went over the fence — yet another example of people back then underestimating the athletic strengths of women.

My success didn't stop at bragging rights; I also earned nearly $16,000 in prize money from "The Superstars." I was very definitely no longer an amateur athlete, and I was glad to have the opportunity to be compensated for my efforts. (I was invited to participate again in 1976 and finished fifth overall, good for an additional $5,000 or so in prize money.)

You can't put a price on meeting those amazing women in person. Plus, I was part of an event that promoted and highlighted outstanding women athletes from 10 different sports.

And in case you're wondering, no, Billie Jean King and I are not related despite having the same last name. But I have long admired her and have met her several times, thanks to "Women's Superstars" and traveling in the same athlete's rights and women's sports advocacy circles for decades.

I can also thank her for helping me improve my tennis game. Several years ago, we were at a formal affair in New York celebrating women in sports. I was in a long gown and super high heels and found myself standing in the wings just off stage next to Billie Jean as we were waiting to be introduced. I turned to her and said, "I'm taking up tennis and I love it."

She turned to me and beamed. "I'm so glad. It's a special game. How are you doing with it?"

"I'm really into it," I replied. "And I think every time I play, I get a little better."

She nodded. And I saw my moment.

"But I am really having trouble with my backhand. Do you think you could give me some pointers?"

She cracked another grin and thus started an impromptu lesson. She asked me to show her my swing, which I pantomimed as well as I could considering the constraints of my spangly dress and stilettos. She asked about my racquet grip and how I approach the ball, and all sorts of other minutiae I would never have thought to pay attention to on my own.

We became thoroughly engrossed in this lesson. I don't know how long we'd been doing that, me swinging, her giving feedback and pointers, but clearly some time had passed. Suddenly, we both got the feeling that we were being stared at. We looked up: Everyone was watching us, and they were laughing or shaking their heads at our irrepressible need to constantly be doing sports, despite having been called on stage to get the event started.

I laughed in response and shrugged. "Did you expect me to miss an opportunity to learn from the best?"

✶ ✶ ✶

Because of my success in diving, I've also visited a fair bit of the world and met firsthand with incredible people from all corners of the globe, including other "superstars" beyond the world of sports.

Perhaps my very favorite travel memories came in 1965, shortly after the AAU National Championship meet held near Toledo, Ohio. Because I did well there, I was selected to be part of a small coterie of swimmers and divers invited to the United Kingdom and Western Europe for an international tour. A very special diving friend, Tom Gompf, was on this trip, too. We visited London and Cardiff and then hopped over to Paris to see the Paris Follies Cabaret performance where we met legendary diver Larry Griswold.

Then, onward we went to Nice and eventually Monaco. There, I met some truly famous people, including the ultra-glamorous Princess Grace of Monaco, formerly Grace Kelly of the silver screen. She received us at her mansion where Tom and I staged a diving exhibition in her backyard pool. I was just in awe. I mean, I had gotten fairly comfortable with being well-known in the world of diving and was a recognizable athlete among folks back home. But to be in the garden of royalty was beyond words.

What's more, the day of our visit, actor David Niven, the

Micki, actor David Nevin, Tom Gompf.

star of "The Pink Panther" and many other films from the 1960s and '70s was also there. This was just an incredible gee-whiz experience. It was one of those moments when I couldn't help but stare and wonder if it was all a dream. I couldn't believe I was standing next to these people who were legitimately world famous.

Our team leader told us before we got off the bus in Monaco that we must leave our cameras on board. It was a "strict order" not to take pictures of Princess Grace and her guests. But not one of us did what we were told. Tom Gompf and I were surreptitiously trying to take pictures of ourselves with our famous hosts in the background, including Princess Grace's husband, Prince Ranier III. We thought we were so smooth and totally getting away with it when suddenly Prince Ranier turned to us and asked for our camera. We were toast — and in big trouble. But instead, the very gracious Prince handed the camera to another person and asked him to take a picture of the three of us.

After our stint at the palace, Princess Grace's brother, Jack Kelly — himself an Olympic medalist in rowing and a good friend of Tom's — took the divers to a restaurant built right into the cliffs overlooking the Mediterranean Sea. It didn't take much encouragement for us to make our way to the restaurant railing, about seven meters high. And yes, without hesitation, the three of us dived off the balcony into the Mediterranean Sea.

The waiters tried to stop us, but Jack Kelly assured them we had the skills to survive, and indeed we did. We put on quite a show for the diners.

But that was just the warm-up. Tom had earned a bronze medal in the 10-meter platform at the 1964 Tokyo Olympics, and in 1970 and 1971, he would become the world champion in diving from 100 feet high. He, of course, wanted to take this stunt even further. Behind the restaurant, there was a cliff edge that was easy to reach. So, naturally, up we climbed.

Looking down from that height — about 55 or 60 feet up — induced a touch of vertigo. I was never the biggest fan of diving from heights, but I was up for this challenge. After that, I could say I'd gone cliff diving, a feat I would duplicate in Acapulco several years later alongside some world-famous Mexican daredevils who dived there for a living.

Though I always felt I dived better from the springboard, there is something enticing and exciting about diving from a higher platform or natural rock cliff into surging surf below. Not for the faint of heart to be sure, and not something I dabbled in regularly, but certainly an experience I was thrilled to have.

Another exciting event came in 1969 when I took part in a military sports championship held in Pescara, Italy. Organized by the International Military Sports Council (CISM), this festival of sport first got started in 1948. In 1951, the United States joined CISM, and now American military athletes could display their athletic talents in international competition.

A 1969 Associated Press article recalled my participation in those games, noting that I was the first woman ever to do so. The AP article called me "a novelty because few European countries have women in their armed services. But she encountered no difficulties. 'The men were really great,' Miss King laughed. 'It was a very ego boosting trip.'"

Indeed, the CISM Games were an opportunity to meet members of other countries' armed forces and interact with them. I was impressed by the shared sense of precision. Perfection and discipline go hand-in-hand.

* * *

My journeys with diving also took me to China for an unprecedented exhibition in 1973 as part of a small group of 10 swimmers and divers dubbed "Friendship Through Sports." This visit was part of a larger diplomatic effort undertaken by the U.S. State Department to improve relations with China. Since the 1949 revolution, which exiled Chiang Kai-shek to Taiwan and installed Mao Zedong as head of the Communist Party, mainland China had been closed to Westerners. A series of crises including the Korean War ensued, further straining diplomatic relations between the U.S. and China.

Mao Zedong, himself an avid swimmer who staged several self-glorifying open water feats during his reign, saw sports as an important component of his ruling philosophy. And in April 1971, the first signs of a thawing of cold relations between the U.S. and China came when China's ping-pong team invited members of the U.S. team to China. The players and an entourage of journalists were the first Americans permitted to enter China since 1949, but they apparently wedged the door open with their paddles on the way out.

In July 1971, National Security Advisor Henry Kissinger (who would become President Nixon's Secretary of State in 1973) made a secret trip to China, after which the United Nations formally recognized the People's Republic of China by endowing it with the permanent Security Council seat that had been held by Chiang Kai-shek's Republic of China on Taiwan since 1945.

This was an enormous political shift, and in February 1972, President Richard Nixon spent eight days in China. The visit helped ease tensions between the two nations, but the relationship was still delicate.

USA team in China. Photo courtesy of Bernie Wrightson.

That's why our trip in 1973, which was sponsored by the National Committee on United States-China Relations, was so extraordinary. We were another example of "ping-pong diplomacy" and the politicians wanted us to help them bridge the gap. I was proud to be among the first Westerners allowed into China in nearly a quarter century, and I was excited as hell. It was an off-the-charts invitation to participate in that tour, and I was pleased to be able to share my love of diving with our new friends abroad.

I learned a lot during that three-week, four-city tour that took us to Guangzhou, Changsha, Shanghai, and Beijing. There were 2 divers and 8 swimmers in the group and 2 coaches: Jim Gaughran, a member of the 1956 U.S. men's water polo team who also coached at Stanford University, and Ingrid Daland, a former champion swimmer originally from Germany who founded Daland Swim School in 1987 in Conejo Valley, California. Al Schoenfield, editor and publisher of *Swimming*

World and *Swimming Technique* magazines, served as the press liaison for the group. His wife Faye Schoenfield also helped with publicity and press. Dick Williams of the State Department was our official escort and interpreter along with Thomas Bernstein of the National Committee on U.S. and China Relations.

We had a great lineup of athletes on the trip, including:

- **Frank Heckl**, a competitive swimmer who'd earned six golds and a silver medal at the 1971 Pan American Games and went on to become an orthopedic surgeon in Albuquerque, New Mexico.

- **Karen Moe**, who won the women's 200-meter butterfly in Munich and was a world-record holder in the same event. She later became head coach of the women's swim team at the University of California, Berkeley.

- **Jane Barkman**, a two-time Olympic champion and world record holder who earned gold in the 4 x 100-meter freestyle relay in Mexico and Munich. She also earned an individual bronze in the 200-meter freestyle at the 1968 Olympics.

- **Steve Power**, the University of Washington powerhouse who took gold in the men's 400 IM at the 1970 World University Games, a.k.a. the VI Summer Universiade, in Turin, Italy, and became a much-beloved age group coach.

- **Mitch Ivey**, a formidable backstroker who took silver in Mexico City and bronze in Munich in the men's 200-meter back.

- **Brian Job**, a standout at Stanford University and bronze medalist in the 200-meter breaststroke at the 1968 Olympics.

- **Ellie Daniel**, the four-time Olympic medalist and record holder whose double-jointedness allowed her to thrash the competition in butterfly events. She broke Moe's world record in the women's 200-meter fly.

- **Lynn Vidali**, a terrific swimmer who took silver in the women's grueling 400-meter individual medley at the 1968 Olympics and won bronze in the 200-meter IM in 1972.
- And **Bernie Wrightson**, a fellow diver who'd earned gold in the 3-meter springboard event in Mexico City.

We dived and swam in a variety of beautiful pools before crowds of tens of thousands of spectators. Various members of the U.S. diplomatic team working to expand the relationship with China were involved in supporting us on our journey including Nicholas Platt, a career diplomat based in China in the 1970s who would go on to become executive secretary of the Department of State. He wrote about our trip in his 2010 memoir *China Boys: How U.S. Relations with the PRC Began and Grew.*

Reading his recollections brought back some funny memories. His description of a culturally complicated exchange between the Chinese women's coach, Ms. Chen, and Ingrid Daland, reminded me that American women had a societal advantage in some respects when compared to our counterparts overseas.

The story — which some might find distasteful — centered around how Western women dealt with menstrual periods while training and racing at an elite level. Coach Chen asked Coach Daland how her swimmers and divers managed this, and the question probably seemed bizarre. American women just use a tampon and move on, naturally.

But for the Chinese women, it was a very important question fraught with centuries of cultural practice; at the time, the Chinese had a strict taboo against putting any object into any bodily orifice prior to death. As Platt explains, "When one dies, body plugs made of a material that accords with your rank — jade for the emperor, on down to wood for the peasant —

are inserted. A tampon, in short, was not only unknown, but unthinkable."

Some serious linguistic maneuvering followed as Platt tried to convey the foreign concept of a tampon to the Chinese women. Eventually, Coach Daland fished a tampon out of her bag and showed them this simple device. The lightbulbs went on, and it seems, tampon manufacturers soon found another emerging market in Asia.

Platt also relates a hilarious story about our farewell banquet, during which we were subjected to an unusual dish — bull pizzle. Now, in American cuisine, the most sensitive bits of a bull seldom make an appearance on the menu, but in Sichuan gastronomy, this dish that translated as "Ox's XXX à la Maison," was considered the utmost delicacy. Wanting to send their esteemed guests off in style with full bellies, it's no wonder this top offering was on the list of local specialties we'd get to enjoy. Uncertain whether this would be palatable to his young charges, Platt expressed concern that the Americans — the women in particular — might balk at the plate.

But, as it turned out, he needn't have worried. As the toasts followed, each bite became more delicious than the last, and then the pizzle landed on the table.

"The meat was cut into long strips and covered with a marinade of vegetables, but unmistakably XXXs to those who knew," Platt writes. But we athletes were blissfully unaware; we had no idea which part of the animal these tender and tasty cuts of meat had come from.

As Platt reports, Karen Moe heartily dug in and was delighted by the flavor of the most special dish. She asked what the meat was, which apparently made the officials a little nervous. "The Chinese officials looked at each other, and the interpreter sitting next to Karen leaned over and replied, in a serious manner, 'It's a very special kind of tendon.'" To which, Karen proposed a toast, and we gladly all drank.

No harm, no foul — it's all just protein, right?

As Platt concludes, the evening — and the trip as a whole — was an "unqualified success." And, our emissary expedition turned out to be a major diplomatic, country-wide undertaking that still reverberates today.

Case in point, David Han was a 24-year-old swimmer in Shanghai when we visited in 1973 and he learned some backstroke tips. An Olympic-caliber swimmer, Han never got a chance to compete because the People's Republic of China boycotted the Summer Olympics from 1956 to 1980. That ongoing boycott resulted largely from the 1949 overthrow of the Kuomintang government and its retreat to Taiwan — a consequential political rift that's still playing out today — and the subsequent squabble over Taiwan's status in the Olympics.

Undeterred, Han cultivated the relationships that began during our trip. In 1980, the U.S. and China staged a dual meet so swimmers and divers from these two top-tier aquatics nations could meet despite having both boycotted the 1980 Games in Moscow. It was there that Han met Don Gambril, the legendary coach of the University of Alabama. Gambril hired Han to assist with the Alabama program, and Han served as the aquatics manager for the city of Memphis until his retirement in 2015. (He passed away in November 2024.)

His son Eddie Han was also a competitive swimmer, who went on to become a physiologist who's worked with the world's best swimmers to help them find those tiny adjustments that can shave off critical milliseconds.

We gave David his first pair of swimming goggles and helped put him and his family on an aquatic trajectory for life.

Similarly, divers Li Kongzheng and Li Hongping also attended the diving clinics Bernie and I staged, and both went on to become Olympians. Kongzheng eventually became the head diving coach at my alma mater, the University of Michigan, and Hongping coaches the USC Trojans. Talk about our efforts coming full circle!

I also wonder about the impact that our trip had culturally; during the 2016 Rio Olympic Games when Chinese swimmer Fu Yuanhui gave a particularly candid poolside interview following a race in which she didn't perform as well as she'd hoped. She cited the arrival of her period the day before as a reason she felt tired and weak, breaking a taboo that crosses many cultures. The young swimmer's statement charmed viewers the world over while underscoring how much Chinese culture has changed since we American swimmers and divers first met with our Chinese counterparts in 1973. I wonder whether Coach Daland's practical orientation around basic feminine hygiene products might have been a catalyst for breaking a longstanding taboo and allowing women in China access to a helpful means of taking care of monthly business.

All told, however, our goodwill tour didn't transpire without controversy. We were warned by the Amateur Athletic Union that our visit would violate FINA's Rule 53 that barred competition with non-member China. FINA, which today is called World Aquatics, is the international governing body for all aquatic sports (swimming, diving, water polo, and artistic [synchronized] swimming). Despite the fact that we were careful not to race or otherwise compete against the Chinese athletes while we were over there, we still got suspended from the AAU and the U.S. Olympic Committee.

But the trip was bigger than sports, and we were OK with the fallout because what we were working toward seemed so much more important than our own competitive desires. In fact, most of us were retired from amateur competition anyway, so the sanctions against us didn't have real teeth.

A couple of weeks after we got home from the trip, we also got disqualification warnings from FINA, but after a little back-and-forth communication (aided by the State Department), the international aquatics body finally saw our point that this had been an important diplomatic venture, and they ultimately did not disqualify us. The State Department praised us for our efforts to promote friendship with China through sports, and it meant a lot to us that we had the backing of our federal government. After all, it was Secretary of State Kissinger who'd first proposed the visit, so it seemed only right that the Nixon administration would have our backs when FINA came calling!

We also set in motion a revolution in Chinese diving that still haunts American divers today. At the time, China conducted their diving program in the dark, but our trip lit a spark. We put on exhibitions, and after each one, we invited interested kids to try diving. They filmed our diving and watched our exhibitions intensely. And, truth be told, this is the origin of the Chinese dominance in the sport of diving.

Taking what we taught them, Chinese divers steadily began climbing in the standings. Today, they are the world powerhouse in our sport. There's no doubt that our visit sparked the fire of Chinese diving, a dynasty that continues six decades later.

We broke barriers with our visit. But we also saw China at its lowest point. They didn't have cars or many of the modern items we took for granted. They travelled on bicycles pulling carts behind them. All of us on the trip were stunned — flabbergasted. It felt like we had stepped back in time when we landed in China.

They say travel changes you, and being able to see another culture and people and how different their lives were from ours made me realize what advantages I grew up with — and how special America is.

The trip was exceptional in so many ways. I did a lot of diving, and I spent time with special Olympic friends. The sights we saw were incredible. And, yes, I learned to use chopsticks. I walked along the Great Wall of China — I have photos somewhere of me sitting on the Wall in my swimsuit!

Madame Mao, the famous Chairman's wife, even hosted us at a basketball game while wearing an elegant dress, patent leather shoes, and a Rolex watch. Her presence signaled that Mao and his cohort welcomed this rapprochement with the U.S., and we were thrilled to be part of this peaceful adventure.

Life in China has changed significantly in the nearly 60 years since I visited, but it was great to experience their culture; even down to the food, it was all strange and exhilarating. What an amazing opportunity to see things and meet people I would never have otherwise.

I really have gotten to see the world, all because of diving.

Micki, sister Lorraine, with Mom and Dad.

King family Christmas in Pontiac.

Micki outdoors.

Mexico City – Team photo.

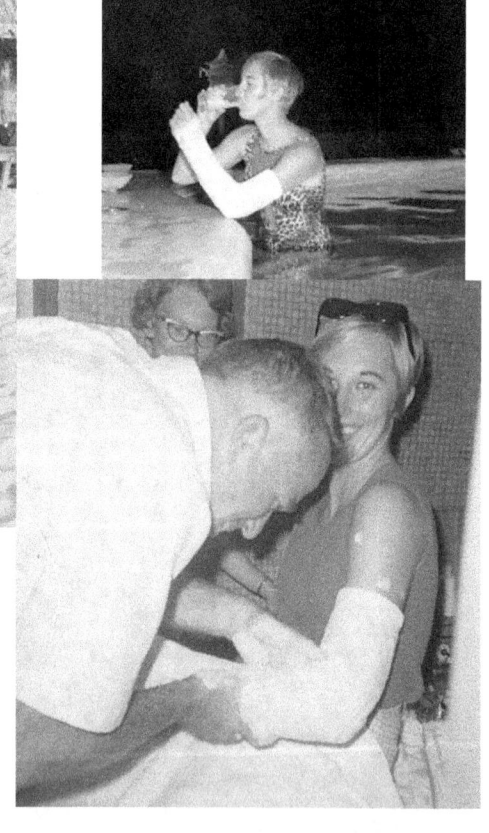

*Mexico City – Micki with
her broken arm in a cast.*

Micki with Munich finishers Milena Duchková of Czechoslovakia and Marina Janicke of East Germany

Micki with her gold medal.

OLYMPIC HEROES

XXth OLYMPIAD-1972 MUNICH

U.S.A.

MICKI KING

Micki's collector's card.

Micki and Dick Kimball being interviewed on television.

Micki with her gold medal.

Micki's collector's cards.

Micki with Chinese divers..

USA swimmers, divers, and staff who traveled to China.

China trip photos courtesy of Bernie Wrightson

Micki with Princess Grace Kelly and actor David Nevin.

Micki playing tennis in Superstar Action photos.

Courtesy Michigan Sports Hall of Fame.

Micki being sworn in at the meeting with President Gerald Ford.

Courtesy Gerald R. Ford Presidential Library, National Archives & Records Administration.

*Micki signing autographs. Requests came in
the mail with return envelopes to send back.*

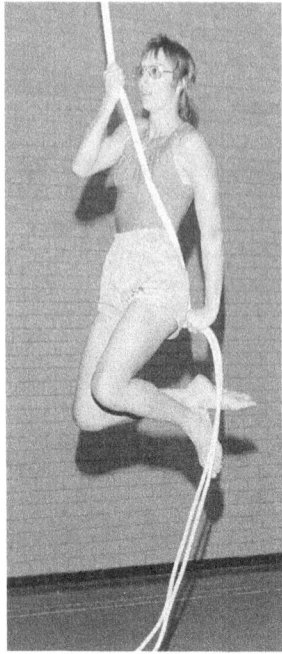

Micki during her Air Force Acadeemy coaching days.

EXCLUSIVE TO YOU IN YOUR CITY

Great form,
Maxine !!! . . .

Showing intense concentration, professional diver Micki King displays the form that advanced her from the Women's Preliminary to the Finals of ABC Sports' "The Superstars," airing **SUNDAY, MARCH 7** (2:00-3:30 p.m., EST), on the ABC Television Network.

Micki King is among the 12 top women athletes who compete in Women's Finals after elimination of 12 other athletes in the Preliminary round.

Micki running in the Superstars event, captured by network photographers (above).

(Left): The photo release and caption from ABC Sports.

PRESS RELATIONS
1330 AVENUE OF THE AMERICAS
NEW YORK, NEW YORK 10019

PHOTO RELEASE

*Micki's Air Force Cadets surprised her
with a fun welcome to a workout.*

*Micki during her Air Force
Acadeemy coaching days.*

Team USA Diving in Seoul, South Korea, 1988.

Air Force activities outside the pool.

*Air Force activities
outside the pool.*

Micki with her children, Kevin and Michelle.

Micki and grandson, Luke, at one of his swim meets.

Air Force activities outside the pool.

Colonel Micki King, USAF (Retired).

Micki's sister, Lorraine, and their aunt
in front of Micki's Hall of Fame plaque.

Micki and her son, Kevin, at a soccer match in London.

Micki and her good friend, Tom Gompf.

Tom Gompf, his wife, Joyce, and Micki.

Micki and sister, Lorraine.

Spindletop Tennis gang, Lexington, Kentucky.

Lorraine, Tom, and Micki.

Micki with her mother and father.

CHAPTER 8

VOICE AND VOTE

"It doesn't matter how strong your opinions are. If you don't use your power for positive change, you are indeed part of the problem."

– Coretta Scott King, author, activist, and civil rights leader

As amazing an experience as the 1972 Olympic Games had been, it wasn't all roses and sunshine for the USA Olympians on many fronts. During the plane ride back to the U.S., we all began comparing notes on our experiences within our different sports. It became obvious every sport had serious issues that were ignored or excused. In short, leadership on all fronts was missing.

It was also obvious that athletes were being railroaded by both local and international politics — Bubba, the boxer whose sweats I'd borrowed for the medal ceremony, for one. A few days after he cheerfully bailed me out, Bubba narrowly lost his bout to a Polish boxer named Jan Szczepański in the third round in a 3-2 decision made by Soviet and Eastern Bloc judges that conspicuously conflicted with how the fight actually went. Szczepański ended up with the gold medal in the men's lightweight division, and Bubba had no recourse to dispute the ruling and no athlete's liaison to appeal to for help. Disgusted with the corruption at work, Bubba turned pro soon after the Games, leaving amateur sports far behind.

Bubba's was just one of many similar stories: Athletes had no input, no voice, regarding any aspect of their sport.

I watched this happening right in front of me, but "accepted" it. We had no voice at the time. That's just how it was, and we followed the leaders. We were pawns and we accepted it.

But during the plane ride home, ideas began to germinate. It became clear that we athletes needed to be heard. Suddenly, we were talking seriously about how we could get involved. What a wild idea, huh? We had no real plan, no objective — we were simply yakking, throwing out issues, problems, and barriers we faced. But were we onto something useful? To answer this question, we needed to know how other athletes felt and we had no inkling where this answer would lead.

It soon became clear we were on to something BIG!

"Amateur athletics" was the environment we were hoping to change. And to understand the context requires a look back at the original concept of amateur athletics and the Olympic movement, which was modeled on the ancient Greek idea of a large quadrennial festival that celebrated the notion of civilization through athletic supremacy.

As amateur sports grew in popularity in the latter half of the 19th century, Charles Pierre de Frédy, Baron de Coubertin, a French academic and historian, decided it was time to establish a modern Olympic tradition that would harken back to the ancient Greek contests that, as some historians romanticized, held such power over the populace, they ended fighting between warring states during each quadrennial festival.

Coubertin helped establish the International Olympic Committee (IOC) in 1894 to bring together leaders from sporting societies around the world. Their objective was to develop and stage the first Games in Athens, Greece, in 1896. Coubertin was opposed to women being involved, and the first Olympics featured only male competitors.

The IOC had two American members — James Edward Sullivan and William Milligan Sloane — who formed a subcommittee to organize a group of U.S. athletes to participate in the festival. Sullivan was also a founder of the Amateur Athletic Union (AAU), which was established in 1888 to provide common standards for amateur sports in the United States.

Sullivan did a lot for amateur sports, but like Coubertin, he wasn't in favor of women competing. So, no women were allowed at the 1896 Games. But, at the 1900 Paris Games, 22 women competed in croquet, equestrianism, golf, tennis, and sailing. American women, however, were not allowed to be among that small group of female athletes.

In 1904 and 1908, nations sent a few women to participate in a very limited number of events. For example, archery was the only event open to women in St. Louis in 1904. Though 45-year-old American archer Lida Scott Howell won three gold medals at that Games, she received little fanfare.

The 1912 Games in Stockholm marked the first time female divers and swimmers could compete, but even then, there were only two swimming events and one diving event for women. Of the more than 2,400 competitors who participated at the 1912 Games, only 48 of them were women. But no American women. We would not be permitted to participate again until the 1920 Games. Perhaps not entirely coincidentally, American women athletes were only finally allowed to compete in the Olympics the same year that women's suffrage became a reality in the United States.

Still, Sullivan held considerable power in athletic spheres, and his efforts to support the growing Olympic movement helped put the United States on a path to Olympic glory. The committee he founded with Sloane also had huge influence over would-be and current Olympic athletes in the United States. That authority continued to grow alongside the flourishing Olympic movement.

At a November 1921 meeting held at the New York Athletic Club, Sullivan and Sloane's subcommittee was formalized as the American Olympic Association and it continued to control American athletes aiming for Olympic participation. In 1940, the AOA's name was changed to the United States of America Sports Federation, and five years later, it was changed again to the United States Olympic Association — the USOA.

In 1950, Public Law 805 passed, establishing the USOA as a private, nonprofit corporation, clearing the way for the organization to fundraise via tax-deductible contributions. In 1961, the group's name changed again to the United States Olympic Committee (USOC) and in 2019, it was updated once more to become what we know today — the United States Olympic & Paralympic Committee.

The USOC — which oversaw all Olympic sports in the United States — was staffed by "executives" who called all the shots for USA athletes. We dubbed them "the Suits" because they were "businessmen" who had no association with organized sports. They worked in the office — not at the track or the pool or on the playing field. That disconnected them from active competition and created a huge gap between them and the current athletes who were dedicated to making the USA Olympic team. Simply put, America's elite athletes were ignored.

So, that's where the Athlete's Advisory Council, the AAC, comes in.

The concept of an "athlete's advisory council" — a group of current and/or recent Olympic athletes — to help guide Olympic sports in the U.S. started gaining traction around the 1968 Mexico City Games, echoing the Olympic Project for Human Rights push for Black athletes' rights. The idea was for USA athletes to stand up for their rights. We knew we were simply pawns that "the Suits" controlled; despite being the key stakeholders, we had no voice, no vote, no representation. This situation resembled how the United States of America became its own independent nation, breaking away from the British Empire for similar reasons — taxation without representation. It was incredible that the needs and desires of elite American athletes had been ignored for decades.

Our sporting lives were directed and managed by "the Suits," and in the 1960s and '70s athletes began to realize this needed to change. Our opinions had never been asked for. And, I'll say it again, getting a seat at "their" table was a radical idea that gathered steam as the '60s gave way to the '70s.

Meanwhile, amateur sports in America were also undergoing a seismic shift. The Olympic Games had a strictly enforced regulation that Olympic athletes must be "amateurs." That meant no sponsorship of any kind — athletes couldn't even have the name of the equipment manufacturer on their gear. Any change to the concept of amateurism would have resounding implications for the international Olympic movement. So, it was against this backdrop that the National Collegiate Athletic Association (NCAA) withdrew its support of the USOC over these brewing political issues that were pounding amateur sports.

Soon, several amateur sports federations withdrew from the NCAA. Similarly, the AAU was in upheaval, in part related to the shake-ups at the NCAA. All this churn created serious concern in elite sporting circles. But, it became the beginning of change within the U.S. Olympic movement. It also began my quest to bring athletes into the room where decisions about our athletic futures were being made.

The U.S. Olympic movement also faced significant challenges regarding the initial awarding of the 1976 Winter Olympics to Denver. This was a huge debacle! The Games had been awarded to Denver in May 1970, but it didn't take long for the Denver Olympic Committee's plan to crumble. Their proposal wildly underestimated how much it would cost to stage those Games. And the sketchy management plan — which included transporting athletes via helicopter to Vail, Steamboat Springs, and other mountain resorts where several events were to take place — turned out to be a smoke and mirrors project. In short, the proposal was impossible and would prove disastrous for Denver.

In an effort to stave off this coming crisis, a motivated group called the Citizens for Colorado's Future gathered 25,000 signatures from Colorado residents calling for a statewide vote to move the Games to another city. The signatures were delivered in dramatic fashion at an IOC meeting before the 1972 Winter Games in Sapporo, Japan. A subsequent Colorado state ballot measure barring taxpayer funding for the 1976 Games drove the final nail in the coffin and Denver withdrew its bid. In the end, Innsbruck, Austria, hosted the 1976 Winter Olympics.

This unpleasant episode highlighted tensions between the IOC and USOC.

Impacts of dysfunction extended to individual athletes as well. Consider the heartbreaking story of Rick DeMont, a young, talented swimmer from California who qualified at age 16 to represent the U.S. in Munich in 1972. DeMont had asthma and had declared to the USOC all the medications he was taking prior to competing in Munich where he claimed gold in the men's 400-meter freestyle.

After the race, he was whisked off for drug testing, as were all medal winners. Several days later, DeMont's sample came back positive for the banned substance ephedrine, which was a component of Marax, his prescription asthma medication. Despite the fact that he had diligently informed the USOC of his use of the medication with the required medical disclosure forms, his participation was never cleared with the IOC's medical committee. Someone had dropped the ball, and DeMont was branded a cheater, despite having done everything by the book.

DeMont was immediately stripped of his medal — it went to Bradford Cooper of Australia — and DeMont was barred from further participation in the 1972 Games. It would take until 2001 for the USOC to admit it had mishandled DeMont's paperwork, but only the IOC has the power to restore his medal; the race results remain the same.

Changes needed to be made to prevent this sort of regrettable and entirely avoidable episode from happening to anyone else.

All of these problems — when presented against the backdrop of the very public terrorist attack in Munich, which played out on live television to the horror of shocked viewers worldwide — tarnished the Olympic reputation. Questions and criticism of what exactly Olympic administrators were thinking, both here and abroad, swirled like synchronized swimmers performing a routine.

As the *New York Times* noted in February 1973, some USOC staff members pointed to "excessive organizational politics, an unwieldy, unrealistic committee structure, an inability to relate to and understand new athletic terms, and attempts by some officers to use their position and influence to enhance their own image, at the expense of more clearly defined goals." The USOC was so messed up, even its staff members criticized the organization publicly.

In short, the Olympic Movement was in jeopardy — change was needed, especially on behalf of the athletes. And perhaps the biggest reason why stemmed from the lack of input by athletes. This directly impacted athletes in many ways including, but not limited to, team rules we'd be required to follow, and coach selection, for example. Such critical components could make or break an athlete's Olympic experience.

On the airplane home from Munich, that proverbial ball for change started rolling. It seems everyone on that flight had experienced something negative related to general incompetence at the USOC, compounded by our lack of voice and vote. For example, track athletes missed their prelim event because the coach could not read the international time clock correctly.

Then there was world-record setting pole vaulter Bob Seagren whose pole was disqualified by the International Amateur Athletic Federation officials just before his event. That ban wasn't even linear, but instead amounted to a rollercoaster of ban, reversal, and reinstatement of the ban. The official reason Seagren couldn't use the fiberglass Catapole he was used to was because it had not been available to all athletes since August 31, 1971.

Despite this setback, Seagren was able to finish second with a pole he borrowed. But he held the world record of 18 feet, 5¾ inches in 1972. Was that borrowed pole he was forced to use the difference between silver and gold? And who was speaking up for athletes caught up in such picky, shifting-rules gamesmanship?

It seemed obvious that giving athletes a seat at the table would help "the Suits" understand athletes and their needs. We weren't sure how many issues there were and how deep they went, but we thought there were surely enough to bring it all to the attention of the leaders. And perhaps our efforts to bring athletes' concerns to the forefront would help the shaky Olympic movement in the United States build a stronger Team USA going forward.

It was clear the time had come to ask "the Suits" for an athlete rendezvous. We had no idea what was ahead. We just knew we all needed to sit down and talk to each other.

At the time, Colonel F. Don Miller (U.S. Army, retired) was Executive Director of the USOC and Robert Kane was USOC Executive Vice President. They agreed to host the meeting.

Historically, the Olympics were military in nature. Archery, javelin, running, and many other Olympic events originated from martial training and maneuvers. The innate nationalism baked into the international festival also echoes military primacy. I certainly wasn't the only Olympic athlete who was also a member of the armed forces; many American athletes and indeed scores of competitors from other countries were also active military personnel whose affiliation with the armed forces enabled our ability to participate.

Thus, it made sense that Colonel Miller and other bigwigs in the armed forces were part of the leadership group of many sporting organizations on the Olympic track. It's also part of why I found myself at the forefront of the movement to push for athletes' rights. My own military affiliation gave me instant street cred with some of the leadership team and a way in.

Buoyed by Miller and Kane's acquiescence to meet with us, a couple of us went to NYC where USOC House was then located and started going through the Olympic yearbooks. We were searching for an athlete from every winter and summer sport to join our "cause." And yep, we picked that initial AAC gang from the USOC winter and summer yearbooks.

We didn't realize at the time what we were building. Our objective was to find a wide representation of U.S. Olympians that included every age, every ethnicity, every state, every educational level, and, of course, every sport. Our intention for this group was to be a cross-section of the entire Olympic cohort.

And we found them.

In September 1973, I sent letters to the identified individuals inviting them to take part in the event and I underscored that the weekend would be <u>free</u>. "The only strings attached involve you as an athlete's representative for your sport to the USOC Athletes' Advisory Council." I further told the prospective members that "We may not solve all the world's sports problems, but I hope you agree it's a L-O-N-G overdue step in the right direction."

None of us were sure what we were getting into — yet. But, the trip was free, and easy to say "yes" to. I encouraged 100% participation, and we very nearly got it — only 6 of the nearly 40 invited athletes declined.

Our first meeting was finally set. And it didn't come a moment too soon. In late 1972, Philip Krumm, a former speedskater and speedskating official, was elected president of the USOC and held that position from 1973 until 1977. His history of involvement with an Olympic sport, as both an administrator and a competitor, gave us hope that he would listen to our concerns. However, the *New York Times* had some reservations, noting in a November 1972 article: "Whether the bespectacled, soft-spoken, 66-year-old businessman is equipped to handle the pressure that awaits the next [USOC] president, after the chaos and confusion at Munich, remains a critical point in the opinion of observers."

We scheduled our first meeting for November 3, 1973, in Chicago. Thirty-eight athletes were invited, and the U.S. Olympic Committee agreed to cover the cost of our attendance. As hoped and planned, the invited group included a representative from each Olympic sport — 21 sports in summer and 6 in winter.

Unfortunately, the representatives from weightlifting, volleyball, judo, men's basketball, and ice hockey weren't able to attend because of prior commitments. But we were thrilled that a whopping 33 other athletes turned up for the meeting. There were 21 men and 12 women, which was representative of the gender balance in Olympic competition at the time.

The average age of the group was 29 — not a group of teeny boppers. This first meeting of the USA Olympians was historic. Hopefully these athletes would be leaders in their respective sports. We expected them to speak up about the experiences of others in their sport and list their specific issues and challenges during this first meeting ever of USA Olympians.

The Chicago meeting was our first time together — we didn't know each other, and the athletes we picked had just one thing in common — we were Olympians. We had no idea where this venture would take us — if anywhere. Truth is, most everyone there that day saw it as a fun and "free" weekend!

But during that first meeting, a warm bond was established — and an atmosphere of understanding — that would see us forge a path forward, together.

We had an incredible lineup of athletes and advocates in attendance:

- **Tenley Albright Gardiner,** who'd won gold at the 1956 Olympics in figure skating along with five consecutive U.S. women's championships. A 1961 graduate of Harvard Medical School, Gardiner went on to practice as a surgeon for 23 years and taught at her alma mater. She also served as chief physician for the U.S. Winter Olympic team in 1976.

- **Frank Shorter,** who dominated the men's marathon at the 1972 Munich Games, besting the silver medalist by more than two minutes. He also claimed silver in that most grueling event in Montreal in 1976. A Yale University graduate, Shorter went on to become an attorney. He helped found the United States Anti-Doping Agency and served as its chairman from 2000 to 2003.

- **Suzy Chaffee,** the Olympic alpine ski racer turned model, actress, and social activist. Chaffee worked hard to get Title IX passed and was the first woman to serve on the board of the U.S. Olympic Committee. She later founded the Native Voices Foundation, an organization that seeks to develop Native American Olympic athletes.

- **Willie Davenport,** the Olympic track and field star who appeared in four summer games (and won gold in the men's 110-meter hurdles in 1968) before becoming a runner for the American bobsleigh team at the 1980 Winter Games in Lake Placid. He very nearly played professional football and eventually joined the Army. He was serving as a colonel in the U.S. Army National Guard when he tragically died of a heart attack in 2002 at just 59 years old.

- **Doris Brown,** the two-time Olympic runner who became the first woman to clock a sub 5-minute mile indoors. She became a running coach and worked closely with the national women's team in the run-up to the 1984 Olympic Games.

- **Kenny Moore,** a terrific long-distance runner who ran the marathon in the 1968 and 1972 Olympics and then spent 25 years as a journalist writing for *Sports Illustrated*. He also published several books and wrote the screenplay for *Without Limits*, a biopic of fellow Oregon runner Steve Prefontaine.

- **Linda Myers,** the 1973 winner of the World Archery Championships at Grenoble, where she helped her team earn a silver medal, and a commercial artist who represented the U.S. at the 1972 and 1976 Olympics.

- **Ellie Daniel,** the world-record-setting swimmer who scooped up three medals — one of each color — at the 1968 Mexico City Games and earned bronze in the 200-meter butterfly at the 1972 Munich Games. An attorney, she serves as a prosecutor with the Los Angeles County District Attorney's office.

- **Steve Genter,** who also won the full rainbow of medals at the 1972 Munich Games in men's swimming. A Pan American champion, Genter was a member of the gold-medal-winning 4x200 meter freestyle relay, swimming third to set Mark Spitz up with a considerable lead and a clear pathway to his historic medal haul in Munich.

- **Russell Webb,** a bronze medalist and member of the 1968 and 1972 U.S. Men's Olympic Water Polo team, who was also a very good swimmer, having won two medals at the 1967 Pan American Games in Winnipeg. He went on to become an oral surgeon.

- **Bill Wright,** the so-called "Black DiMaggio" who played centerfield for 10 seasons in the Negro Leagues and another 10 years in the professional Mexican League. Baseball wouldn't become an official Olympic event that awarded medals until 1992, but several exhibitions had been staged to advocate for its inclusion beginning in 1900. Having been discriminated against by the Major Leagues because of his race, Wright knew all too well what it meant to be an overlooked athlete, and his insight was important for us to include.

- **Dixie Woodall,** a three-time AAU All-American and member of the USA Women's 1967 Pan American Games silver-medal-winning basketball squad. Women's basketball wasn't added to the Olympic roster until 1976, but Woodall went on to become a renowned coach at Seminole Junior College and Oral Roberts University. She coached the USA squad at the 1977 World University Games in Bulgaria to a silver medal.

- **Edward Williams,** a 1964 graduate of Dartmouth who competed in cross-country skiing and was twice named All-American. He served in the U.S. Army and took up biathlon, representing the U.S. in the 1968 Winter Olympics in Grenoble, France. A 1974 graduate of Columbia Law School, Williams would go on to become the second chairperson of the AAC and serve as assistant U.S. attorney for the Southern District of New York.

- **Harry Petersen,** a member of the 1972 Olympic bobsledding team representing the United States in Sapporo, Japan. He also represented the U.S. Navy bobsled team throughout Europe during his competitive career. Petersen, who graduated from the University of New Hampshire, served in the U.S Navy for 26 years and retired as senior chief in 1992.

- **Jesse Valdez,** an All-American AAU boxer who was named the top welterweight amateur boxer in America in 1972 and earned a bronze at the 1972 Munich Olympics. The two-time National Golden Gloves champion was also an Air Force guy who made a career out of the military. He never boxed professionally.

- **Marcia Jones Smoke,** a fellow Michigander. The three-time Olympian earned a bronze medal at the 1964 Tokyo Olympic Games in the K-1 500 meter sprint canoe race. She also earned three golds at the 1967 Pan American Games and set a record by earning 35 national championships and 24 North American titles.

- **John Allis,** a Princeton University grad who made waves overseas in the hyper-competitive world of road cycling at a time when many Europeans thought American riders were constitutionally incapable of competing with them on two wheels. He rode in the 1964 Olympics in Tokyo and represented the U.S. again in 1968 and 1972.

- **Rob Ridland,** an equestrian and jumping specialist who competed at the 1976 Montreal Olympics and won several grand prix competitions throughout his lengthy career. Ridland, who holds a law degree from Columbia University, was also heavily involved in the governance of riding sports, serving as a board member of U.S. Equestrian and the United States Equestrian Team Foundation.

- **James Melcher,** a Columbia University épée fencer who represented the United States in Munich in 1972 after having clinched gold and bronze medals at the 1971 Pan Am Games. Melcher went on to found a capital management firm and a macro global hedge fund.

- **Peter Gilbert,** one of only three U.S.-born members of the men's field hockey team that competed in the 1971 Pan American Games in Cali, Colombia. (The team didn't finish high enough in that tournament to earn a berth in the 1972 Olympic Games.) Gilbert was a substitute delegate, attending on behalf of Hans Zucker. At the time of the meeting, Gilbert was vice president of the Long Island, New York-based Gilbert Manufacturing Co. that made electrical wiring devices. (Hans Zucker had been a member of the 1968 Olympic field hockey team.)

- **Linda Metheny,** an artistic gymnast who represented the U.S. at the 1964, 1968, and 1972 Olympics. She also won seven intercollegiate championships while studying at the University of Illinois. She became a national and international judge for the sport.

- **Kathleen Roberts-Homstad,** who, at just 16 years old, competed in the 1968 Winter Olympic in the luge and then returned for the 1972 and 1976 Games. Over the course of her illustrious career, Roberts-Homstad won more than a dozen U.S. and North American championships. She also had the best finish by an American woman in the first 20 years of American luge.

- **Loren Drum,** an Air Force captain from Omaha who competed in the modern pentathlon in the 1970s and was a member of the 1972 Olympic pentathlon team. Drum served as the first secretary of the AAC, and we have this incredible all-around athlete to thank for such scrupulous record-keeping that helped me remember the minute details of our earliest days with the AAC.

- **Larry Hough,** a rower who competed in the coxless pairs at the 1968 and 1972 Olympics. He and his partner, Tony

Johnson, won silver in 1968. Hough went on to become a successful venture capitalist.

- **John Writer,** an incredibly accurate shot and three-time All-American at West Virginia University who earned silver in the 50-meter free rifle 3x40 in 1968. He then nabbed the gold in the same event while setting a world record at the Munich Games in 1972.

- **Sandy Shellworth Hildner,** the 1967 U.S. alpine skiing champion who attended the University of Colorado, Boulder, where she trained with the men's ski racing team under coach Bob Beattie. Despite a bad leg-break the same day she won the U.S. National Giant Slalom, she rehabbed and was selected for the 1968 Grenoble Olympic skiing squad.

- **Mike Elliott,** a three-time Olympic Nordic skier who served as an infantry officer in the U.S. Army. He was deployed to Vietnam and was awarded the Combat Infantryman Badge, the Vietnam Gallantry Cross, and the Bronze Star Medal for that service. He was also a member of President Gerald Ford's Presidential Commission on Olympic Sports and worked hard to build the sport of cross-country skiing in the U.S.

- **Steve Gay,** a member of the men's 1972 U.S. Olympic Soccer team who went on to coach the UCLA men's soccer team from 1975 to 1979. He also played professionally in the North American Soccer League in 1975 and was inducted into the National Association of Intercollegiate Athletics Soccer Hall of Fame in 1977.

- **Dianne Holum,** a speedskating prodigy who in 1966 became the youngest person to compete in the world speedskating championships. Two years later, at the tender age of 16, she won the silver medal (in a three-way tie) in the 500-meter race at the 1968 Winter Olympics in Grenoble, France. Four years after that, she picked up the gold in the 1500-meter event while setting an Olympic record. She also won a silver medal in the 3000-meter race that year. She retired from competition soon after that at just 20 years of age, but stayed in the sport, coaching 14-year-old Eric Heiden to five gold medals at the 1980 Winter Games in Lake Placid.

- **Richard Abrahamson,** an Oregon native and basketball player who was drafted by the Phoenix Suns in 1969. Abrahamson became a handball player and competed at the 1972 Olympic Games. In 1976, he served as captain of the U.S. men's handball team in Montreal. He later joined the U.S. Army and served as a first lieutenant in South Korea. He was a staunch advocate of athletes' rights and contributed so much to our efforts on the AAC.

- **Wayne Baughman,** a three-time Olympic wrestler and ultra-endurance athlete from Oklahoma who earned 16 national titles and never placed lower than third at any national event. Baughman was also a military guy and colleague who served as the USAF's head wrestling coach from 1976 to 1984 and 1989 until 2006. He's the only person who's won national championships in all four recognized wrestling styles — collegiate, freestyle, Greco-Roman, and Sambo.

- **Carl Van Duyne**, a New Jersey native and sailor who competed in the Finn event at the 1968 Summer Olympics. A two-time silver medalist at the Pan American Games, Van Duyne also served on the President's Council of Sports and sadly died at age 36 of cancer.

I opened that first meeting, of what would come to be called the Athletes' Advisory Council (AAC), of course, with a thank you, a welcome to all, and an explanation of the concerns raised on the plane home from Munich. I thanked Mr. Kane for allowing us to meet and for covering the cost for us to come together. And I summed up my opening remarks with the following: "I want to know if you all agree that U.S. Olympians should have a 'voice AND vote' in all matters regarding our participation and our representation as a USA Olympic team member."

And, you know what their answer was.

Then, each athlete introduced him or herself and talked about the sport they were representing and some of the issues they were seeing among their teammates that had been ignored by administrators. The comments were eye-opening, and one response I particularly remember was about "team curfews."

Team curfews are valid, of course. Olympic athletes don't — won't — argue with a coach about a curfew. But, apparently there were coaches who kept strict curfews on athletes even after their event was over. We could all relate to the frustration of not being allowed freedom from "team rules" after our event was over. "Hey, Coach! This is the OLYMPICS! I'm done! It's over for me! I'm off now to enjoy the Olympic Village, see the city, meet friends at the Hofbräuhaus!"

You get it. Yes sir, no sir... three bags full (of s---t). No voice, no vote by the Olympians was the rule back then. Sitting together in Chicago now, we had no idea if we'd be heard or if we'd ever meet again. But it soon became clear our concerns were valid, and needed to be addressed. Yes! We were onto something big.

And we had some bigwigs backing our efforts; after we completed the discussion of team problems, United States Senator Mike Gravel of Alaska addressed the Council, outlining what he thought were the strong points in favor of passage of a bill he was co-sponsoring to support athletes. After Senator Gravel completed his presentation, we had an open discussion of the proposed bill.

We talked for about an hour and then took a vote to see where opinions were leaning — we voted 30 to 3 in support of the establishment of an Amateur Sports Board. We were unanimous in voting for the establishment of a sub-committee to study the USOC and its make-up, constitution, by-laws, management, and sub-organizations. We were also unanimous in backing the idea of establishing a National Sports Foundation to provide more development money for athletes and athletic facilities in the U.S. To facilitate the work of the AAC in pushing for better and more harmonious relations with the USOC, we agreed to meet at least quarterly going forward.

After a busy morning, we adjourned for lunch and had a chance to chat with each other. In the afternoon, I called for a show of hands from the group — I wanted to know whether my colleagues felt the meeting was of enough importance that they would have attended if it hadn't been all paid for by the USOC. I was pleased when 19 of the 33 athletes present indicated that they would have attended under those circumstances. The other 14 members said their only hesitation was financial.

We then moved on to additional business. Suzy Chaffee reported on the 10th Olympic Congress that had been held in Varna, Bulgaria, a month prior. That meeting had produced several additional points of interest that the AAC would champion including:

- Bringing IOC eligibility rules up to date
- Urging the IOC, the International Federations, and the National Olympic Committees to consider the inclusion of women in their membership and commissions
- Exploring how those three bodies could have closer contact with athletes
- Encouraging government support for the development of sports

It was an incredibly productive meeting and a wonderful chance to connect with athletes from across the Olympic sports spectrum. Some of the larger sports, such as track and field, had a larger membership share, which we thought only fair. These athletes were representing their teammates, and that representation should be proportional to the number of athletes impacted by that representation, just like the House of Representatives of the United States.

Our objective with that first meeting was to simply confirm yes or no that the concerns voiced on the plane home from Munich were valid, present among all teams, and did indeed need serious attention. It was critical that we had input from Olympians in the room — especially winter athletes who obviously were not on the ride home from Munich.

The answers to all our questions were loud and clear: Yes, yes, yes! Within the first 15 minutes, it was undeniable that we'd hit a home run. But we had no idea what that weekend would turn into.

During the lunch break that day in Chicago, one of our athletes passed by Phil Krumm who was speaking to another "Suit." This athlete overheard Krumm say, "Those kids are really getting ramped up. We created a monster by allowing them to have this meeting."

CHAPTER 9

GAINING MOMENTUM

**"Courage calls to courage everywhere,
and its voice cannot be denied"**

– Millicent Fawcett, British political activist and writer

Diving is a sport ruled by physics. Gravity, momentum, propulsion, lift, and drag all play a part in every move a diver makes. And, if you're aiming to slip gravity's bonds — even for the moment it takes to execute an inward 1½ somersault — you'd better understand the fundamental rules of how objects move and act upon each other in space.

These laws govern all aspects of our lives, whether we realize it or not. Sir Isaac Newton's laws of motion come into play every day both literally and figuratively. And that proved to be true for our fledgling Athlete's Advisory Council (AAC).

Newton's first law states an object at rest remains at rest and an object in motion remains in motion at constant speed in a straight line — unless acted on by an unbalanced force, a.k.a. inertia. This is perhaps the most obvious law the AAC encountered. With the launching of the AAC, we athletes became the unbalancing force that pushed the USOC to make significant changes: including how we conducted business and how they would deal with their long-established reluctance to include athletes in decisions affecting their own Olympic ambitions and goals.

Newton's second law states acceleration of an object depends on the mass of the object and the amount of force applied. But it quickly became apparent as our group grew and gained steam that we were gathering momentum. Former, current, and would-be Olympians across the spectrum of sports followed our efforts closely and expressed gratitude that their concerns were finally being addressed for all to see. We became a force for change.

Newton's third law states whenever one object exerts a force on another object, the second object exerts an equal and opposite force on the first. This became apparent as we hit snags and challenges along the way. Despite the generally positive reception that first AAC received when we were given permission to meet, the law of action and reaction means not everyone wanted athletes at the table. And, yes, we faced significant challenges in cementing athletes' voice and vote in Olympic proceedings.

Challenges surfaced quickly after the creation of the AAC. The National Governing Bodies (NGB) were not happy with the idea of athletes having a voice and weren't prepared to accept 20% athlete representation on their respective boards of directors. One NGB even sought to have its athlete-elected AAC rep removed from the AAC! Happily, this challenge was defeated, but this, of course, proved we were on the right track.

Our proposal also included that seven athlete representatives join the USOC board of directors. Not everyone was happy about that. In short, we needed to be at the table when the big decisions were being made, right?!

One of the rules of AAC membership stated that those involved must have competed within the two most recent Pan-American or Olympic Games to be eligible to represent their sport at the AAC. This would ensure our membership remained abreast of all the issues facing current Olympic and Pan-American athletes. It also ensured that athlete reps rotated regularly, which kept our membership up-to-date and current. The leadership couldn't perpetuate itself, which was one of the complaints we had with other sports governing bodies in the U.S. at the time.

In all, the AAC had six primary areas of focus:

1. Defining amateurism

2. Providing athletes with Games preparation and logistical support

3. Involving athletes in administering team and staff selections

4. Improving communication among the many stakeholders — including the U.S. Olympic Committee, the National Governing Bodies, the athletes, and the public

5. Improving athlete safety at the Games through medical research and employing best practices for helping athletes reach their peak performance

6. Raising funds to support athletes in their quest for Olympic gold

It's hard to overstate how critical this financial piece is to Olympic and would-be Olympic athletes. Case in point, in 1972, the U.S. received an invitation for divers to travel to Russia for a competition. Exchanges with Russia back then were rare, and the invitation was enticing. The Russians would pay for everything once we were in country. But we had to get ourselves there. There was no money in the diving fund at the time, but we needed the international competition experience. So, we accepted the invitation. But we had to select divers who could afford to pay their own way, who weren't necessarily the best athletes we had. Government funding could conceivably make those sorts of issues disappear overnight.

The AAC also focused on improving equity for female athletes. Rick Abrahamson, a handball player who competed in the 1972 and 1976 Olympics, was charged with leading that discussion at a May 1975 AAC meeting. In his research, he noted that, "It is felt by women participants in the 1972 Olympic Games that the USOC Sports Committee and the AAU are often more concerned about chaperons and femininity than performance. The AAC recommended filling all chaperone spaces with qualified female coaches, trainers, or medical personnel as most appropriate."

Abrahamson's report also noted that even after the passage of Title IX — which intended to improve women's access to opportunities in higher education, including athletics — the USOC was behind the times in supporting women. "Presently, there is a general feeling of athletes that the USOC is doing pathetically little to assist female participation in sport and is not providing the equal opportunity that is a women's right. Each must have the opportunity to excel in athletics and to reach her fullest potential," he wrote.

We hoped the AAC would help solve such problems across this broad spectrum of big and small challenges. We sought to bring attention to them while creating more opportunity for female athletes, a difficult-to-establish ideal.

Looking back through the documents that came out of this era, I'm reminded that while the passage of Title IX in 1972 was a watershed moment for women athletes, it didn't always work as intended. It wasn't like a switch was flipped and suddenly women were on equal footing with all men in all sports circles. In fact, at most schools, the enforcement of Title IX backfired and removed athletic opportunities for men! Oh, the law of unintended consequences!

But why did it backfire? Well, the federal law known as Title IX says the number of college women athletes must be in proportion to the percentage of women enrolled at the school. So, if a university's enrollment is 50% women and 50% men, then the number of women athletes in that school needs to be the same as the number of men. That seems fair, right?

Statistically, universities and colleges in the United States have about 5% to 10% more female students than male students. So, this means, by law, there must be more opportunities for women athletes in most U.S. colleges today than for men.

But, wait! There's more! If a school must add another sport to get into compliance with Title IX, how do they decide what sport to add? Well, Title IX has a provision called "interest and ability," so, a university cannot randomly add a new sport. For example, an Athletic Director can't just add a women's volleyball team if women students aren't interested in volleyball. Instead, the athletic department needs to find out what fits the "interest and ability" of their female students. This is a key part of the law that states the college must conduct a student survey for input about which new sports to consider. When I was assistant athletic director at the University of Kentucky, we did research like this.

So the million-dollar question is: Are universities today actually meeting the requirements of Title IX — a federal law!

Very few schools are, it turns out.

Title IX laid the groundwork for change, but "the law" can only reach so far and the revolution is far from complete. There is still so much work to be done to elevate women's sports to the same level as men's sports.

For sure, some sports have evolved to a point of near-parity. For example, the Women's National Basketball Association and the National Women's Soccer League now routinely get the prime-time media coverage they so richly deserve and fans are super excited about how these sports have grown and their growing presence. But there are so many other sports that haven't advanced as much as they should have by now. It's fair that each sport has its own historical arc and will progress at its own speed, but I do believe that more can and should be done across the board to foster expansion of women's sports — both professional and amateur.

But, of course, so much of it comes back to money and how much each school is willing to spend to add opportunities for women. Many universities that have the big football and basketball teams you watch on TV bring in truckloads of money from those sports, but it's mostly men's sports that are the major profit centers. Women's sports teams — even the women's March Madness teams — simply don't produce the revenue that a Big 10 football powerhouse team can. I am hoping that in time, that fact will evolve, but at the moment, men's sports are the tried-and-true money-makers, and as in all other aspects of life, money talks.

That said, I think the institution of Name-Image-Likeness rules that now allow student-athletes to monetize their athletic pursuits will impact college sports and participation and that could hold implications for Title IX and opportunities for women in sports going forward. How exactly it's going to shake out remains to be seen, but anytime there's big money involved, you can expect that something is going to shift.

My point is, we should never take for granted that Title IX happened and that means all's honkey-dorey with women's sports. Far from it. This work isn't finished and we need to protect and advance the movement for more opportunities for girls and women in sport. We need to keep maturing the push that Title IX started in a direction that allows all women to have access to sports and to continue to thrive.

Sometimes I worry that the younger generations don't really

know what we went through to create these opportunities and how different life was for athletically-inclined girls and women prior to the passage of Title IX. Case in point: I recently spoke at a girls' high school awards ceremony. After the talk, two young ladies came up and asked me what Title IX was! I was astonished and reminded that we need to continue to ensure women's inclusion in the world of sports.

In building this unfinished revolution, we were also trying to transform how society and women themselves saw their ability to participate in sports. Back in my day, women weren't supposed to sweat — that was reserved for men. The AAC and the Title IX movements both wanted to eradicate that outdated thought pattern and encourage girls and women to venture into sports. The only way to find out how good they could be was to try, and we were all for that effort. We knew many female athletes could be as good if not better than their male counterparts, and we wanted them to excel to bring more gold home for Team USA. We knew the next Olympic superstar was among the scores of girls who'd been told it wasn't ladylike to be an athlete. We were determined to make that concept history.

✶ ✶ ✶

I was humbled to be a part of this growing movement for athletes' rights. But it wasn't easy work, and there were plenty of growing pains along the way. Straight away, the USOC paid mostly lip service to us and didn't take us seriously. At that first Chicago meeting in 1973, they told us they were glad to have our input. Their first questions were, "What color boots do you want for the march-in ceremony?" And, "What sport should be the first to march in?"

Talk about a complete misunderstanding of our objectives! We responded with, "Are you kidding me? We're not talking about uniforms, we're talking about legislation!" It was a lot of work and constant pushing to get the USOC to understand that we wanted much more than just a vote on the color our opening ceremonies uniforms.

It was July 1975, when there was finally good news to report to the AAC athletes. We'd made progress in getting the USOC to agree to our requests for:

1. An Athlete's Bill of Rights

2. New ByLaws

3. A "Broken Pay" proposal to help athletes secure financial support from their employers while training for Pan-American or Olympic Games

About 30 companies had already agreed to continue paying their athletes who were selected for an Olympic team. And for those whose employers didn't, the USOC would provide financial assistance, not to exceed $400 per month with an additional $50 per month per dependent. This financial support was an incredible help to athletes training for the Olympics.

We also succeeded in convincing "the Suits" to change how the AAC elected its members. The Board wanted nominations from the field and also wanted elections by the USOC Board. But, we won and elected our representatives without the Board's oversight.

We also ensured that athletes would have the transportation, food, housing, and training sites they needed at competitions and be made fully aware of all USOC services available via a guide book issued for each Games. Getting adequate medical support from doctors with a sports medicine background was another key move we made to ensure athlete safety and success. We created uniform standards and other apparel rules for international competitions. And we moved to make all aspects of the Games equal for male and female competitors. This included everything from where they could train to the size of the medals awarded — there was a time when women's medals were smaller. Of course, we wanted women to have the same experience as men across the board.

Coaching selection was another crucial issue for the AAC. We moved to ensure the best coach was selected to support the athletes, rather than the "most connected" coach. We also worked hard to ensure more female coaches were involved; it didn't make sense that a male coach, with no background or experience in coaching women, would be assigned to female teams.

One sticking point — athlete participation on the USOC board — took much longer to work out. In 1975, the USOC Board agreed to have 20% athlete representation on the Board. However, up until 2022, the Suits determined who those athlete representatives would be. Not exactly the voice and vote we were hoping for, but better than not having any athletes on the board at all. Finally, in 2022 swimmers Donna de Varona and John Naber became the first two board members elected by the athletes.

All of these things were important, but I think the Athletes Bill of Rights was arguably the most critical issue we worked on, and we wordsmithed that document until it perfectly put athletes' rights at the center of the AAC's efforts and the USOC's attention. Athletes' rights was our primary goal. We were for real.

Finally.

Because of my role as AAC chair, I was deeply involved in the push for the Amateur Athletic Act, which led to a few brushes with the highest government officials in the land, including Senator John V. Tunney, a Democrat from California. He sponsored the Amateur Athletic Act, an important piece of legislation, that the AAC worked hard to get passed.

As part of those efforts, on November 5, 1973, I testified before the Committee on Commerce of the United States Senate about the need to change amateur status in the United States.

I would be lying if I said I wasn't nervous. Our Athletes' Advisory Council was so new, and the stakes were very high as we tried to get off the ground. And here I was standing before the Senate Commerce Committee preparing to speak in support of the bill proposed by Senator Tunney. (I'm so glad I went to the restroom before I spoke!)

Alongside me were big wigs from the NCAA, the AAU, and the USOC. I cleared my throat and told the collected dignitaries:

"We, the athletes, are expected to win everything but are given little or no help to do it under the present system. Today, with this hearing, we end years and years of communications gaps between athletes and administrators. We were finally asked what we think, and we are telling you now. Please do not expect continued excellence from our USA athletes unless you give us Government support. The athletes want the bill."

We sure did. As I told the Committee, we had received an overwhelming response from the athletes we'd contacted about the Act, and at our first AAC meeting two days before that Senate testimony, our 33-member group had voted 25 to 4 in favor of supporting the Amateur Sports Act, which was signed by President Carter in 1978.

Some said it was long overdue. Others said they couldn't wait. The athletes overwhelmingly wanted to see calculated change directed toward building American sports from the grassroots level. And we all simply wanted to begin immediately to support our USA Olympic athletes.

"The group that I represent is unprecedented in history," I told Congress. "We are pioneers. We are hungry to be heard, and we feel the attempt to combat the provisions of the Amateur Athletic Act are very weak."

We wanted sports organizations to be accountable to someone other than themselves. At the time, governing bodies lacked credibility because there wasn't appropriate oversight — this led to nepotism and other problematic practices.

Kenny Moore, an Olympic marathon runner who competed at the 1968 and 1972 Olympics, also testified that day, and told the Committee that the Tunney-sponsored bill would help end "a repository of incompetence," a phrase his fellow runner Frank Shorter often used to describe the mismanagement of sports administration in the United States — namely at the AAU, NCAA, and USOC.

We put it all out there during the hearing, but as with anything government related, the wheels of progress turned slowly.

Finally, by 1975, there was more good news: That June, President Gerald Ford established the President's Commission on Olympic Sports (PCOS). Created by executive order, the commission was formed "partly in response to the continuing conflicts among various organizations involved with amateur sports in this country and partly in response to declining performance by the United States in international competition such as the Olympic Games." President Nixon had first floated the idea of such a PCOS to help navigate the thorny issues growing in amateur sports in America, but it finally came to pass when President Ford proposed using reprogrammed funds from the Department of Health, Education, and Welfare to fund the Commission.

The PCOS, which was split into four divisions, was staffed by Executive Director Michael Harrigan, who was responsible for overseeing all staff activities and serving as a liaison between the staff and Commissioners. Harrigan had been a collegiate athlete and had previously served as a consultant to the White House and the President's Council on Physical Fitness and Sports. He was also a Presidential staff assistant.

John A. McCahill, Esq., directed the legal division of the PCOS. He had served as assistant to Special Counsel James D. St. Clair during the Nixon impeachment hearings. The legal division studied and reported on all legal and financial aspects of U.S. Olympic sports organizations and would help with drafting and passing any legislation that might result from the group's efforts.

Beverly L. Dobb led the communications division, which was responsible for managing the flow of information to the public and other parties.

Kent A. Maxfield led a team of six consultants and two assistants in the research division. They studied each of the 27 Olympic sports' structures, activities, and governing organizations and investigated non-governing organizations such as the Boys Club.

Lois Finkelstein served as the office manager and liaised between the PCOS and the Department of Health, Education, and Welfare while also supervising clerical staff.

The PCOS consisted of 13 presidential appointees, four congressmen appointed by the House Speaker, and four Senators appointed by the Senate President Pro Tem. I was pleased to be one of the athletes named to the PCOS. The other appointments were athletes or other leaders who were involved in amateur or professional sports in some capacity, including:

- Gerald B. Zornow, Commission Chairman and Chairman of the Board at Eastman Kodak Co. He had been a professional baseball player and college football player.
- J. Glenn Beall Jr., Republican Senator from Maryland.
- John C. Culver, Democratic Senator from Iowa.
- Donna de Varona, Olympic gold medal winner in swimming.

- W. Michael Elliot, a national cross-country ski champion and U.S. Army infantry officer who served in Vietnam.

- Barbara Ellen Forker, director of women's physical education at Iowa State University.

- Jerome H. Holland, president of Hampton University and a director of the New York Stock Exchange who served as U.S. ambassador to Sweden from 1970 to 1972. He was also the first African-American to play on Cornell's football team and was named an All-American in 1937 and 1938.

- Lamar Hunt, president of the Kansas City Chiefs football team.

- Rafer L. Johnson, 1960 Olympic decathlon gold medalist.

- Jack Kemp, Republican Congressman from New York and a former professional football player.

- James A. McCain, Kansas state commissioner of labor.

- Ralph H. Metcalfe, Democratic Congressman from Illinois and a member of the 1932 and 1936 U.S. Olympic teams who earned one gold, two silver, and a bronze medal in Olympic competition.

- Robert H. Michel, Republican Congressman from Illinois.

- Norman Y. Mineta, Democratic Congressman of California.

- Howard K. Smith, a news commentator and analyst for CBS and ABC.

- Ted Stevens, Republican Senator from Alaska.

- William A. Toomey, 1968 Olympic decathlon gold medalist.

- Ernest M. Vandeweghe, a member of the U.S. Olympic Committee on Basketball and a former professional basketball player.

- Willye White, Chicago State University's women's track coach and a five-time Olympian who scooped up two silver medals.

- Charles "Bud" Wilkinson, former football coach at the University of Oklahoma and special consultant on physical fitness for Presidents Kennedy and Nixon.

The first phase of the PCOS's work involved the study and evaluation of the USOC and other sport membership groups as they related to international competition. That resulted in a report submitted to President Ford on February 9, 1976, by the PCOS, which contained several serious findings:

- Team USA was being outpaced by many countries.

- Amateur sports in America were not getting equal attention with professional sports.

- The conflicts that had arisen between the AAU, NCAA, and USOC clearly affected athlete development in the United States.

The report called for arbitration to resolve disputes and protection against unreasonable restrictions on athletes' rights to compete. It also recommended that national governing bodies undergo a certification process — where more financial resources would be identified and distributed to support Olympic athletic development.

Even in that very initial stage, the PCOS's findings mirrored what the AAC had been pushing for over the previous two years.

The sport-by-sport evaluations completed in the second phase of the PCOS's work resulted in a "Final Report of the President's Commission on Olympic Sports," presented to President Ford on January 13, 1977. That two-volume, 613-page document called for changes that included:

- The creation of a Central Sports Organization — a revamped USOC.

- Resolution by arbitration of jurisdictional disputes among the AAU, NCAA, USOC, and other sports bodies.

- Protection of athletes' right to compete in any Games.

- More funding.

- Organized training and rules for development of elite athletes.

- Use of military personnel and facilities to support Olympic athlete development.

- Establish programs to better develop women's athletics.

- Establish sports for athletes with disabilities.

Again, the PCOS's findings and suggestions echoed exactly what the AAC was pushing for.

One of the most interesting pieces of that final report was the comparison drawn between foreign and American athletes and how we were working at a distinct disadvantage because our government hadn't committed to support us as other countries did. For example, in outlining the potential role of the U.S. military in amateur athletics, the report singled me out.

> Olga Korbut practices her gymnastic routines as a lieutenant in the Russian Army, although she has no other apparent military duties. In fact, a majority of the athletes on the Russian Olympic team are members of the Soviet Military.

> Captain Micki King of the U.S. Air Force spent a significant amount of duty time preparing for the 1972 Olympics in Munich, where she won the Gold Medal in three-meter springboard diving. Unlike Korbut, however, King had other military duties and saw herself as an officer with career potential. Herein lies the difference between the role of the U.S. military in support of international

amateur sports and the role of the military in many other countries.

Certainly many countries view participating in international amateur sports as an instrument of national policy. Accordingly, military forces in these countries view development of world class athletes as part of their mission.

The Armed Forces of the United States have chosen not to adopt this posture toward international amateur athletic competition. Neither the U.S. Congress nor the President has charged the military with this mission, nor has the military chosen to adopt a more active role in international amateur athletic competition within the authority granted it under existing statutes.

I mean, when you put it that way, no wonder we were lagging behind the Soviet military-athletic machine! And this is just one example of the value the PCOS generated in shining a light on the sticky issues facing American Olympians at a time of great upheaval within amateur sports in America.

Meeting President Ford in the White House.
Courtesy of the Ford Presidential Library

Being involved with this high-powered and important group meant a lot to me. After all, President Ford was an athlete and a Michigan guy, and I got to know him a little — I sat next to him at a couple meetings and naturally we got to talking about Michigan and everything else. It was an amazing experience to be involved in this intensive and momentous undertaking.

The PCOS's work eventually led to the passage of the Amateur Sports Act of 1978. This act established the USOC as the coordinating body for USA Olympians and all Olympic-path athletic activities in the United States. It further codified that athletes would have a voice in the governance of Olympic sports in America. The act included modifications to the definition of amateur sports, opening the door to sponsorships and funding opportunities for athletes. It also included a robust Athletes' Rights section, which was written by Ed Williams, the lawyer for the NCAA; Michael Scott; and the lawyer for Ted Stevens on the Senate Commerce Committee, Garry Johansen. The Act also allowed U.S. professional athletes to compete in the Olympics.

In short, athletes' needs and interests were now protected by law!

The problems the athletes on the flight home from Munich had brought into the open were now solved to some extent. Yes, athletes finally had "voice and vote" on decisions that directly affected them. To be sure, progress wouldn't always be linear. But what in life ever is? We had made big changes that directly impacted American athletes for the better.

My last meeting as Chair of the AAC took place on March 13, 1977. I would, however, remain a member of the group as the "past president." I handed the reins over to Ed Williams, biathlon's representative on the AAC.

Being a pioneer in the advancement of amateur sports in the United States was demanding, stressful, and sometimes scary. Ed now took over my post as AAC chair, and he was perfect for the job. At the time, he was serving as an assistant U.S. attorney in the Southern District of New York. So, he had two important credentials — a winter sport athlete was the leader now, and we had an attorney who didn't charge us!

During Ed's term as president of the AAC, the Amateur Sports Act of 1978 became law and the United States boycotted the 1980 Olympic Games in Moscow — two very momentous happenings within the Olympic movement.

My work with the AAC and supporting Olympic athletes wasn't limited to current competitors; I also worked to develop an athlete alumni association with an aim to rally Olympic alumni into supporting and staying involved when they retired from competition. I became the first president of the Olympic Alumni Association, and I loved staying involved.

As I readied myself to move on to my next Air Force assignment in Arizona, I thought a lot about the giant leaps that first AAC accomplished. We established the serious need for athletes' rights and we earned the attention of people outside of sports — the public, the politicians, the sponsors. That first AAC pulled back the curtain and revealed to the world the huge problem that existed all along. Remembering how we opened this door in support of American athletes makes me cry and smile at the same time.

Looking back, I'm really proud of my work with the AAC. I led the team that proved athletes needed a voice, and in the end, our first AAC proved we knew how to use this voice going forward. My Olympic colleagues and I took a deep dive into murky waters and came up with a treasure of "golden" opportunities that continues building champions today, decades later.

But, for athletes past and present, the challenges kept coming — as they always do in this dynamic, never-static world — with perhaps the most difficult chapter in American Olympic history waiting just up ahead.

The Cabinet Room
September 9, 1975

/ The President

/ F. David Matthews, Secretary of Health, Education, and Welfare

Members of the President's Commission on Olympic Sports

/ Gerald B. Zornow, Chairman of the President's Commission on Olympic
    Sports and Chairman of the Board of Directors of Eastman Kodak Company

/ Donna de Varona, former Olympic swimming gold medal winner, ABC-TV
    Sports Commentator

/ Michael Elliot, former member of the U.S. Cross Country Ski Team and
    six-time National Cross Country Ski Champion

/ Barbara Forker, author of articles on women's athletics and recipient
    of honors for work in education

/ Lamar Hunt, President of the Kansas City Chiefs

/ Rafer Johnson, 1960 Olympic Decathlon Champion

/ Micki King, Olympic diving gold medal winner

/ Howard K. Smith, ABC-TV news commentator

/ Dr. Ernie Vandeweghe, team physician for the Los Angeles Lakers

/ Willye White, former member of 5 U.S. Olympic track teams

/ Charles "Bud" Wilkinson, former Special Consultant to Presidents Kennedy
    and Nixon, former football coach at the University of Oklahoma,
    Chairman of the Board of Planned Marketing Associates

  Senator J. Glenn Beall (R-Maryland)

/ Senator John C. Culver (D-Iowa)

/
  James McCain, President of Kansas State University

/ William Toomey, 1968 Olympic Decathlon champion

SEPTEMBER 9, 1975

Office of the White House Press Secretary

NOTICE TO THE PRESS

President's Commission on Olympic Sports

The Cabinet Room

(Clockwise from the President)

> The President
> Micki King
> Jack Kemp
> Bud Wilkinson
> Michael Elliot
> Richard Stone
> Dr. Ernie Vandeweghe
> Cong. Metcalfe
> Dr. Barbara Forker
> Lamar Hunt
> Congressman Michel
> Secretary Mathews
> Senator Culver
> Willye White
> Senator Stevens
> James McCain
> William Toomey
> Donna deVarona
> Howard K. Smith
> Rafer Johnson
> Gerald B. Zornow

Courtesy Gerald R. Ford Presidential Library, National Archives & Records Administration.

CHAPTER 10

TECTONIC GEOPOLITICS

"Many of life's failures are people who did not realize how close they were to success when they gave up."

— Thomas Edison, American inventor and businessman

In the wee hours of Christmas Eve 1979, Soviet tanks rolled into Afghanistan. It was the first time the Soviet Union had invaded a country outside the Eastern Bloc, drawn by a raging civil war and the opportunity to expand its territory in the strategically important central Asian nation.

The 30,000 Soviet soldiers arrived in Kabul to stage a coup, killing the Afghan head of state, Hafizullah Amin, who had only seized power in October, and installing Babrak Karmal, a Soviet puppet leader.

Naturally, the United States looked on with growing concern as its primary Cold War adversary meddled in Afghanistan. Though President Jimmy Carter and his team had hoped cooler heads would prevail, it became clear Moscow was intent on digging itself into the mountainous country. The Soviets were headed for more than nine years of grinding Islamist insurgency and would eventually leave the country after a costly fight — according to some historians, the Afghanistan debacle led directly to the collapse of the Soviet Union.

But before that could happen, the Carter Administration denounced the invasion with everything it had, and that included putting American athletes — prepared to represent the United States at the 1980 Moscow Olympics — in the crosshairs of political brinkmanship. In mid-January 1980, the administration announced it would join Russian dissident Andrei Sakharov in setting a one-month deadline for the Soviet Union to pull out of Afghanistan, or face consequences that included the loss of support by President Carter to send an American team to the Moscow Olympics.

By that time, I had been transferred to Tacoma, Washington, and was stationed at McChord Air Force Base, in the shadow of Mount Rainier and the Cascade Mountains. I was the public affairs officer at McChord, so every time you read in the Tacoma newspaper, "according to an Air Force spokesperson," well that was me. And, I was keeping a close eye on a potential U.S. Olympic boycott as the Carter Administration waited to see if the Soviets would bow to the growing chorus of international voices calling for them to stop their aggressions in Afghanistan.

Just like all the USA hopefuls, I held my breath waiting for news about what would happen next. No one knew for sure if this boycott idea would grow legs, so the summer Olympic sport National Governing Bodies and the USOC forged ahead with their previously scheduled team selections. Everyone hoped Carter was just bluffing and American athletes would have "their moment" later that summer — just like they always had.

In February, the International Olympic Committee's 82nd congressional session opened in Lake Placid, New York, the site of the 1980 Winter Games. USOC leaders — by order of federal officials — were pushing hard for an "international boycott" of the Moscow Games and/or moving the Games to another, less controversial location. Discussion was heated and tempers flared. But the USOC was unable to convince the IOC that the Games should be cancelled, moved, or universally boycotted. The IOC committed to the Moscow Olympics as planned.

Sadly, IOC leaders were also unable to persuade the USOC leaders that their promise of a boycott should be a bluff. On March 21, 1980, Carter declared the U.S. team would not go to Moscow, but the USOC would still hold a formal vote about the boycott a few weeks later.

Six days after Carter's announcement, Mount St. Helens, a massive volcano less than two hours north of McChord AFB where I was now stationed, started grumbling, producing a series of problematic blasts that made it challenging for our Air Force planes to take off. Imagine volcanoes erupting in your neighborhood — yeah, damn scary. Plus, each rumble triggered more requests for information from my office. Of course, the fear on the base was the mission-readiness of our aircraft fleet.

As the pressure built inside Mount St. Helens, so did the Carter Administration's commitment to the Soviet boycott. The USOC scheduled a vote regarding participation in the Moscow Games for April 12, 1980.

I flew to Colorado Springs and was in the room when Vice President Walter Mondale addressed the USOC prior to the boycott vote. I'll admit I wanted to be there in person to understand exactly what was happening AND to make my opinion known. President Carter's "potential mistake" that day would be historic. I made sure I was there.

Tom Gompf — the 1964 men's 10-meter platform diving bronze medalist — was there, too. In fact, he encouraged me to show up. He said we need well-known people who are going to attract attention to the boycott vote, so I dropped everything to get there. My role as a past president of the AAC also compelled me to be in the room for this monstrous vote.

Tom and I have been very close friends for decades, and we had a lot in common, between diving, military service, and a dedication to athletes' rights.

Tom served in the Air Force, too, and he understood the pressure on me to do as ordered by the U.S. President, our Commander-in-Chief. I wasn't willing to vote for the boycott, but it was clear what my boss at McChord expected me to do.

The U.S. President's involvement in the boycott made it sticky and more challenging for us leaders within our sports because everyone knew the Administration could defund the USOC if it voted against the President and sent Olympians to Moscow anyway. Given how hard we'd worked over the previous decade to ensure government funding and support for Olympic sports and athletes, the possibility of losing that funding and all the advances we'd made was devastating.

But as an unwavering advocate of athletes' rights (and an Olympic medalist), Tom also deeply understood that athletes had absolutely nothing to do with this ham-fisted Carter boycott. Tom understood the athletes were caught up in the fallout and they would be punished by the boycott for something totally out of their control. I was so glad we would be sitting together when Carter made his announcement.

Vice President Walter Mondale addressed the group, speaking at length about using the boycott to make a strong statement against Soviet aggression. This was the height of the Cold War, after all, and the USSR was our arch enemy. There was no ambiguity about the request: President Carter and his administration wanted us to boycott the Moscow Games. The Feds were always looking for ways and reasons to poke the Russian Bear, and this bloodless boycott appealed. It would not lead to loss of American lives and, they pointed out, it might actually save both Soviet and Afghan lives.

But the whole idea ran so counter to the ideals the USOC prided itself on, which Tom eloquently told the group when he spoke that day. He explained that the spirit of the Olympic Games rose above geopolitics. In ancient Greece, warring factions reportedly laid down their arms to take part in the festival, rather than pursue animosities. And, in the past, the U.S. condemned other countries that had leveraged the Olympics to make political statements, always insisting the Games were apolitical. To be sure, Olympic history is pockmarked with incidents of nations jockeying for dominance, both on the court of play, and in the world order, proving the Olympics has never truly been free of petty politics. But that's not the aspiration of the movement and that intention is significant.

Nevertheless, allowing the United States government to enforce a boycott to condemn a sovereign nation's invasion of another country just didn't make sense. Especially when it was wildly unfair to Olympic athletes and would give the Soviets an easy path to Olympic medals. Talk about collateral damage! Tom urged the delegates in attendance to vote "no" on the boycott measure.

The Carter Administration's representatives didn't see things the same way. I know for Tom — an airline pilot on an international route at the time — the mere suggestion that his passport could be revoked as punishment for voting certainly held his attention.

I was in a similar position as an active member of the military. President Jimmy Carter was my Commander-in-Chief. There was no telling what kind of reprimand I would face back at McChord when I voted against his wishes.

It seemed we were in something of a pickle.

In the meantime the Athletes' Advisory Council had discussed at length how to deal with the boycott we knew the President wanted, and eventually the AAC developed a workable solution. It was designed to balance the Administration's desire to make a statement while preserving the athletes' rights to compete in Moscow.

The AAC proposed that athletes be permitted to compete in Moscow on the condition they wouldn't stay in the USSR. It might seem a little crazy, but a close look at the map revealed that it could work — the athletes could shuttle from Stockholm, Helsinki, or another location beyond the Soviet empire, that would be more agreeable to the Administration. This way, Moscow and the USSR wouldn't benefit from any income where American athletes were living or any tourism dollars. The Olympics generate lots of money for local businesses, and the American team is often the largest group and the one most likely to spend freely. This financial boycott would hit the Soviets where it hurt most — their wallets.

The proposal also stipulated that American athletes would not stay for the award ceremony for any event. They would compete and leave immediately — even if they medaled, they would not climb the podium. Clearly, empty podium spots would send a very loud message to everyone watching. Theoretically, for Americans who took gold, the American anthem would play and the flag would rise, but with no person atop the podium. Their absence would make a strong statement.

Athletes on the AAC saw this plan as a win-win: "the Suits" would get their political statement and the athletes would get their opportunity to compete. We felt the plan balanced both political and athletic interests.

But, the idea was never put on the table. The Administration wouldn't even hear us out. Instead, they brought the matter to a vote without considering the point of view brought by the athletes' representatives.

There were ten of us representing aquatic disciplines during the vote, and three of us chose to say no to the boycott: Me, Tom, and water polo's representative, Burt Shaw. We felt we must uphold the values of the Olympic movement and what the Games were intended to be — a celebration of the best the world has to offer. We couldn't align with the idea of forcing our U.S. athletes, who had worked so hard for their Olympic opportunity, to be stripped of that chance. They might never get another one. As someone who missed out on a medal in an Olympics I thought would be my only Games, I couldn't accept the thought of benching those athletes and simply hoping they'd make the team in 1984. That's not how life — or sports — works.

I voted my conscience, and I'm proud I stood up for those athletes, even if it didn't matter in the end. Once the votes across all sports were counted, 75% of the 300 delegates in attendance voted in favor of the boycott. We were vastly outvoted, and the boycott went forward; 466 American athletes who qualified to compete in the 1980 Moscow Olympic Games, were abandoned. About 220 — nearly half — of them **never** had another chance to represent the United States on their sport's most prestigious stage. Their sporting careers imploded that day.

∗ ∗ ∗

Back home again, Mount St. Helens finally blew her top on May 18, 1980, belching out a noxious cloud of heavy, iron rock particles. Literally tons of this stuff landed on the wings of the airplanes and the vital equipment on the base, requiring a massive response to scramble those planes away from the disaster.

When Mount St. Helens blew, my office staff and I stayed in constant communication with the public about everything going on at the base. It was scary as hell and historic, too. Everyone on the base was pressed into action to save the fleet while we naturally worried about breathing in toxic particles that might kill us all. There was a lot of confusion and chaos in the moment, and it took a while for things to return to normal.

Both the literal fallout from the Mount St. Helens eruption and the figurative fallout from voting against the Olympic boycott were overwhelming.

Anita DeFrantz, a rower who'd earned bronze in Montreal, led a protest group of athletes by bringing a lawsuit against the USOC. DeFrantz served on the AAC with me and was a staunch athlete advocate who'd been integral in the push for the Amateur Sports Act of 1978. She became an attorney in 1977. Her input was critical to our case, which we were sure had merit. But it was dismissed outright; her suit never got its day in court. Since then, Anita has spoken out about the death threats she faced for those actions.

I, too, paid a price for voting my conscience on behalf of the 1980 Olympic team; apparently my vote was akin to refusing a direct order from the Commander-in-Chief.

When I returned to McChord I was ordered to the base commander's office — my boss. He told me he was appalled to hear I openly voted against the President's wishes. I had expected this from him, but it got worse. Later that year, I was passed over for promotion.

Regardless, I never regretted how I voted that day. And I continue to stand by my decision to vote against the 1980 Boycott.

★ ★ ★

In hindsight, many historians now agree with our stance — that the boycott did nothing to censure the Soviets. It just gave them an opportunity to win a bunch of Olympic medals that would have gone to American athletes. We'd have been better served to face them on the court, in the pool, and on the track than simply stay home.

I'm sad to say a very promising diver, Megan Neyer, the 15-time U.S. National Champion, was among the Americans forced to miss the 1980 Games. Megan surely would have brought home a pair of diving gold medals, had her Olympics not been stolen from her. She had handily won Trials in both the springboard and platform, and she won the springboard World Championships in 1982. She won a record eight NCAA diving championships and was recognized as an All-American eight times. Megan is still the all-time winningest collegiate diver — male or female — in NCAA history. But she never got a chance to show her skills on the Olympic stage.

Sometime later, the Olympic Committee issued a proclamation that stated anyone who'd qualified for the 1980 Olympics as part of Team USA could call themselves an Olympian, even though they couldn't compete in Moscow. It was a nice gesture, but it was just words. There would be no replacing those lost Games, and so many of those athletes never had the opportunity to soar in Olympic competition. My heart ached for them.

I still believe this whole fiasco was one of the saddest periods in Olympic history.

CHAPTER 11

FROM A HIGHER PLATFORM

"Micki King is a self-described liberated woman. However, while other women's libbers fret over being called Miss or Mrs. or Ms., she has solved the problem with Capt."

— Reporter Bill Verigan writing in, "Will AAU Salute Capt. King with Sullivan Award?" Daily News (New York) 26 December 1972

In 1974, *Talon*, the cadet magazine of the USAF Academy, ran an article about me written by Mark Fowler, a 1977 Air Force Academy graduate. During the interview, he asked me "Which fields, if any, do you feel should be closed to women?"

At the time, there was a lot of debate about whether women should be allowed in combat, so I took questions like Fowler's often. Most people refused to respond, but to me the answer was simple: None.

"I think none of them should be absolutely closed. Women should be given the chance to compete for any job on an honest basis, and honestly weeded out if they can't handle the job.

How can you know if a woman can do it if you don't give her a chance to try?" I told him.

I was glad I'd had the challenges I did, and I was proud to have succeeded in so many arenas where women previously had been excluded or were under-represented. And I wanted to ensure that women after me would have the same chance to prove themselves and make a mark in any field they chose to pursue. My opinion was straightforward: Give women a chance. In the Air Force I demonstrated I could do the task I was assigned. Why shouldn't every other woman have the same opportunity?

This is the reason I was drawn to the Air Force. It offered me the chance to have a lifelong career and at the same time pursue my Olympic dreams — the best of both worlds. Despite the passage of the Equal Pay Act (EPA) of 1963, equal pay for women was not widespread in the 1960s.

What I didn't realize that day I joined was the extraordinary opportunities my Air Force career would provide outside of diving. It offered me the chance to establish several precedents starting with becoming the first woman to fill a faculty position at the Air Force Academy. I was also proud to be the first woman to coach a male athlete to an NCAA title in any sport when Rick McAllister won his NCAA championship in 1974.

I also benefited from the Air Force's policy of rewarding excellence; in 1983, I was reassigned to the Air Force Academy as assistant athletics director. Besides my new duties as an assistant athletics director, I headed to the pool every afternoon to coach the diving team. I now had women divers, too, as the school had opened its doors to women cadets starting in 1976.

In all, I was named NCAA coach of the year three times and coached 11 All-Americans, including two women cadets with three national titles between them.

During my second tour at the AFA, I was promoted to Colonel. And ironically, this rank promoted me out of my Air

Force Academy job in the Athletic Department. For the second time in my career I needed to relocate from Colorado. Where would I land on this last duty assignment before I retired? I was asked my preference and my quick response was an ROTC Detachment where I could continue to work with students as I did at the Academy. I had several university ROTC locations to pick from, and I selected Detachment 290 at the University of Kentucky.

Why Kentucky? Location, location, location! Specifically, Interstate I-75 runs from my home state of Michigan through Kentucky down to Sarasota, Florida, where my parents had retired. It was the perfect place for me to finish my career. And the work was a little déjà vu — remember my very first assignment was the ROTC detachment at the University of Michigan 22 years earlier.

So once again, I packed up and made a move, this time with my kids in tow. When we moved to Lexington, they were 7 and 5 years old. They didn't truly understand what it meant to move — to leave the only home they'd known. They could tell it was a big deal though, and Lexington became their hometown as they grew up. We enjoyed many, many years in Lexington.

In 1992, I retired from the Air Force. I'd gone in thinking I'd work out my four-year commitment, but the opportunities the Air Force offered me were too good to refuse. I ended up retiring as a full colonel after 24 years of service.

But I was still young and ready to keep working, so I launched my second career as the assistant athletics director at the University of Kentucky in Lexington. I took up tennis again, too. Billie Jean had inspired me, and I still play regularly today.

In Lexington, I played with a group at Spindletop, a historic mansion that was built in 1935 by the widow of oil baron Miles Frank Yount, who'd made a fortune drilling for black gold in Beaumont, Texas. When Yount died suddenly at age 53, his wife Mildred decided to move to Kentucky and establish Spindletop

Farm on 800 acres of land. It cost $1 million and took two years to build.

The property was acquired by the University in 1959, and now is home to the University of Kentucky Alumni Club. Spindletop also serves as a fancy event venue.

This expansive property has gorgeous tennis courts that overlook vast pastures of the rolling bluegrass that Kentucky is world famous for. Horses graze there, and over the years, I lost count of how many times I watched those spectacular four-legged athletes frolicking in the grass as my two-legged athlete friends and I smacked the ball back and forth across the net.

In many ways, my time in Kentucky was idyllic. I made a slew of friends, and had a fabulous time playing tennis.

Over the 14 years I worked at UK, I helped ensure our student-athletes got the support they needed. I oversaw five sports, and I was able to leverage my insider's knowledge of sports in helping UK student-athletes to succeed in the Southeastern Conference (SEC).

The University of Kentucky — situated as it is in Lexington, the horse capital of the world — didn't have a college equestrian team. Yes, it is an expensive sport, as horses and stables aren't cheap. But there are breeders nearby, and local horse-industry alumni likely eager to support this. Maybe someday...

＊ ＊ ＊

Long after I stopped competing in diving, I continued breaking ground for women in athletic circles and was pleased to give back by volunteering in various capacities to the sport that had given me so much.

In 1990, I became president of USA Diving and was — you guessed it — the first woman to do so. My term ran for four years and it was an honor to lead the National Governing Body of USA Diving.

By design, the term for every president of USA Diving falls within an Olympic cycle. My Games was the 1992 Barcelona Olympics. What a special gem that Olympics was! The diving events were held at the Piscina Municipal de Montjuïc with the stunning, Catalonian skyline forming a dramatic backdrop. That year, the innovative camerawork captured the breathtaking beauty of our sport as 100 divers from 31 nations practiced their craft in the sultry Spanish air, high above the city. It is one of the most beautiful Games I've ever had the pleasure of witnessing up close.

In fact, a now iconic photo of 13-year-old Fu Mingxia captured the aesthetic so stunningly, that it formed the cover of a special Olympic edition of *TIME* magazine. That image, captured by the then largely unknown British photographer Bob Martin, demonstrates a perfect dive, suspended in that one glorious Olympic moment before claiming the gold medal. Prior to snapping that photo, Martin had worked with the Olympic organizing committee and British diver Tracey Miles to perfect the shot; the organizers built a small scaffold to Martin's specifications to get the exact camera angle he needed to capture the incredible image he'd envisioned. Though Miles hadn't qualified for the Olympics that year, Martin captured the extraordinary view of her, sleek and red-suited, soaring against an other-worldly blue sky with Gaudí's Sagrada Familia scraping the heavens beneath her. It's one of the most astonishing images ever rendered of competitive diving.

The Barcelona setting was superlative. Unfortunately, in aggregate, the American diving team's medal haul was not. By 1992, the era of Chinese dominance of the sport had begun and China led the way in Spain. However, individual American divers did perform well. Mark Lenzi — the University of Indiana phenom who was the first diver to ever score over 100 points on a single dive in competition — absolutely trounced his competitors in the men's 3-meter springboard. He took gold by a margin of 31 points!

Scott Donie, the 1990 Southern Methodist University graduate and three-time National NCAA Division I champion, earned a silver in the men's 10-meter platform. Penn State diver Mary Ellen Clark took bronze in the women's 10-meter, a feat she would repeat in 1996 in Atlanta. These extraordinary athletes earned the U.S. the second-most medals overall in diving at the Barcelona Games. Of the 12 medals, the United States took home three, trailing only China, who'd scooped up five — three golds, one silver, and one bronze.

It was such a privilege for me to support those divers in my role as USA Diving president, and I was proud to have been elected to that position. But I realize now it was just another step in a lengthy journey toward bettering opportunities in sports that was made possible — you guessed it — all because of diving.

When I think back, I'm astounded by how many Olympic Games diving has enabled me to attend and how my role morphed from athlete to volunteer to enthusiastic spectator over the decades. It's true that having opportunities to volunteer and be involved with their community is at least as good for the person volunteering as it is for the individual or community they're assisting, and I believe being a dedicated volunteer and avid participant in lots of groups and activities across my adulthood is part of why I'm still healthy and engaged in my 80s.

In all, I've been lucky enough to attend 10 Olympic Games, starting with my unexpected two turns as an athlete.

But my role and Olympic experiences have continued to evolve — and what a treat to be able to remain involved in the movement in so many different ways long after I'd retired from diving myself.

At the 1976 Montreal Olympics, I took a turn in the media booth, acting as a diving commentator for ABC. I had worked as a broadcaster at Pan-Ams in Cali, Colombia, in 1971 and dabbled in it over the years. But truth be told, my Olympic diving teammate Cynthia Potter was much better at it than me, and

I realized I needed to go in a different direction. I did the right thing, and I have so thoroughly enjoyed watching Cynthia cover diving on television over the years! Cynthia and I have remained close all these years. We have the same passion for our sport and serve on a foundation to help USA diving clubs continue their work training USA divers to be the best.

The Team USA boycott in 1980 meant I didn't attend the Games that year, but in 1984, when the Olympics returned to America, I was absolutely in attendance. By then, I had my two small children to introduce to the Olympics. Michelle had been born when I was stationed in Germany, and Kevin arrived two years later. I happily pushed them around in a stroller as I visited the various Los Angeles sporting venues as a spectator — my first time in that super fun, low-responsibility role. Even cooler, Olympic alumni who attend the Games as spectators get some big perks. In L.A., this included access to Olympic House, where fellow athletes reunited and celebrated the Olympic spirit on American soil after the heartbreak of Moscow. Getting to reconnect with folks I hadn't seen in eight years and having my own children in tow made the L.A. Olympics extra special.

In 1988, I was back to serving in an official capacity at the Seoul, South Korea, Olympic Games. I proudly volunteered as Team Manager for USA diving, and that meant I had a lot of responsibilities from making sure athletes turned up at their practices and events on time and enforcing curfews to serving as the divers' liaison to other coaches and organizations. It was a demanding role that turned downright scary when veteran Olympian Greg Louganis, arguably the best diver to ever grace the sport, hit his head on the board during the prelims of the springboard event.

This was my fifth Games, and I understood the challenge and anxiety of being an athlete on that knife's edge between possibility and peril. Plus, having also hit the board during an Olympics, I had plenty of empathy for Greg's situation and was seriously concerned for his welfare as he was being treated deckside.

But like a true champion, despite opening a deep gash in his head, Greg got right back on the horse and went on to win gold in both the springboard and platform events. His two golds were the highlight of the USA diving. On the women's side, Kelly McCormick took bronze in the springboard and Michele Mitchell and Wendy Williams earned silver and bronze in the women's platform event. We may have come second to China in the overall standings, but I was proud of these athletes and the grace with which they handled themselves in tough competition.

I volunteered again in 2000 at the Olympics in Sydney, Australia. I was so excited to visit such an exotic location, and I was happy to pitch in wherever Team USA needed me. I spent time helping at Olympic House, which was great because I got to meet many other Olympic alumni. But I also had plenty of time to see many sports events and just be a tourist in Sydney.

I revisited my happy spectator role in 1996, when the Games came to Atlanta, in 2004 when the Games returned to their birthplace in Athens, Greece, and in 2012 when my son Kevin came with me and we visited my sister, Lorraine, who lives in London.

I loved attending the Olympics with my son, but my daughter, Michelle, Kevin's older sister, couldn't make it. Michelle was married to Allan, an Air Force officer we called AJ. They were expecting their second child in October 2012. Their first kiddo, Luke, was going on five years old, and he watched those London Olympics on TV with his Mom and Dad at home. Little brother Oliver arrived two months later. Today, the boys are into sports themselves including soccer, cross-country, track, and swimming. Tragically, we lost AJ much too soon to cancer in the summer of 2023. Michelle and the boys have healed their grieving hearts, in part, through their respective sports (Michelle played collegiate tennis at the United States Air Force Academy) and the communities they have built within them. Sometimes life doesn't go as planned and sports may suddenly seem meaningless; however, they can also help you transcend life's challenges by providing a crucial outlet for physical, mental, and social needs. Bonding over shared experiences and moments brings us together. We continue to carry AJ in our hearts and make the best of everyday.In thinking back, I realize that all in all, I'm very lucky. Having such a lengthy history of Olympic attendance is an incredible thing that's all because of diving. But even bigger than that, I'm reminded that I'm so lucky to have the love of my family, too.

Meeting Hillary Clinton in Atlanta at the 1996 Summer Olympic Games.

*Michelle and Kevin,
Micki's daughter
and son.*

Michelle, husband, AJ, sons, Luke and Oliver.

*Oliver
and
Luke.*

EPILOGUE

"Diligence is the mother of good luck."

— **Benjamin Franklin**

In June 2024, I traveled to Knoxville, Tennessee, to watch a new crop of Olympic hopefuls compete for a chance to represent the United States on the world stage in Paris at the 2024 Olympic Games. Today's rising luminaries give me hope for the future of diving in America.

Athletes like Kassidy Cook and Sarah Bacon, who wowed the crowd and the judges with their 3-meter synchronized diving prowess; Andrew Capobianco, a silver medalist in the 2020 Tokyo Olympics; and Carson Tyler, who became the first American since 2000 to qualify for the Olympics in both the 3-meter and 10-meter in the same year, all carry on a tradition I'm proud to have played a role in building.

I also enjoyed watching Jordan Skilken dive. Her dad, Steve Skilken, was a 3-time All-American diver at OSU in the 1970s and a friend from my era — the diving world is small! But, the trials in Knoxville attracted an audience of past USA Olympians, including, Lesley Bush, Tom Gompf, and Cynthia Potter. Jordan, who just graduated from the University of Texas, retired from diving after the Trials.

It was so special when Lesley Bush asked me to introduce her at the Rings of Honor Award ceremony. Rings of Honor is the USA Diving Hall of Fame. I was very touched that Lesley would ask me to do the formal presentation at the awards. It was a moving testament to our lifelong friendship.

Lesley earned the gold medal in women's 10-meter platform diving at the 1964 Olympics in Tokyo, following a long line of American women divers who'd topped the event starting with Caroline Smith in 1924.

But Lesley's story of winning that 1964 gold medal is nothing short of astounding, because she was virtually unknown prior to qualifying for the Olympics. She wasn't expected to medal — "the darkest of dark horses," she once said — in part because there wasn't a pool with a platform tower to practice on near her home in Princeton, New Jersey. Instead, she had to travel to Indiana to train during the summer leading up to the '64 Games.

In 1986, Lesley was inducted into the International Swimming Hall of Fame. So...It was long overdue that USA Diving recognized Lesley's talent and legacy. As I thought about what I would say to introduce her at the Rings of Honor ceremony, it struck me how the sport of diving has provided so many opportunities throughout my life to join with others and be part of something bigger than myself.

Surrounded by the other retired divers and watching as the young athletes jumped and jack-knifed at Trials, one word popped into my head: Camaraderie. Even though diving is an individual sport, there is a big team element. Sure, I competed against my teammates, but we were also part of the same team. As Olympic athletes, we all worked to bring glory to Team USA. And when one of us succeeded, the whole team won, too.

It's healthy to be in competition, but it's also healthy to set rivalries aside after the meet is over. That's what camaraderie is all about for me, and seeing my teammates at Trials — the hugs, storytelling, and laughter that followed — reminded me of the special bond we've all forged through diving over the years.

As I looked around at my teammates watching the young

stars spin, twirl, and support each other, it dawned on me that my life in diving has come full circle, in a sense. Remember that first Trials experience in 1960, when other divers were so lavish with their praise, that I started to believe I could advance to the finals? That crop of young stars we were watching were just as encouraging to each other. What a special sport we're part of, and what an extraordinary community we've built. I'm humbled to have had a small role in creating diving's legacy.

The young women diving in Knoxville never had to sneak into the pool to practice, and I'm proud to have been among those who broke barriers and opened doors for girls and women athletes. But I certainly wasn't solo in this push for expanding women's options and helping us gain parity with men.

The list of my fellow groundbreakers is impressive and I can't even begin to name them all here. The problem with lists is, *who did I forget to include?!* Someone is always left off who should be included. All the same, I deeply admire these women who've changed the world through sports over the decades including Billie Jean King, Donna de Varona, and Anita DeFranz. I've talked about them all previously, but some other amazing pioneers who deserve a shout-out here include:

Carol Brown, a Princeton rower who earned Olympic Bonze at the 1976 Montreal Games and competed at the 1984 L.A. Olympics, but was forced to miss the 1980 Games because of the boycott. She was part of the gold-medal-winning U.S. coxed four at the Henley Royal Regatta in 1981, the first year women were allowed to compete in that august competition. She was also a member of our first AAC.

Cathy Rigby, an Olympic gymnast who was part of the "Women's Superstars" program with me. What an impressive, all-around athlete! She became a celebrated actress and used that platform to shatter taboos; she became the first celebrity to endorse a feminine hygiene product when she appeared in a series of TV commercials for Stayfree Maxi Pads.

Cindy Stinger, a 3-time Olympic handball player who worked for the U.S. Olympic & Paralympic Committee for many years. She eventually became manager of the U.S. Olympians & Paralympians Association and has served as a board member with Sportswomen of Colorado and the Olympians for Olympians Relief Fund. She served as executive director of the AAC in the headquarters in Colorado Springs and was the glue that held us together.

Donna Lopiano, a past chief executive officer of the Women's Sports Foundation and is now a top executive and influencer in women's sports. She served as director of women's athletics at the University of Texas–Austin, and is a past-president of the Association for Intercollegiate Athletics for Women. Once a national softball player, Dr. Lopiano is now recognized as a foremost national expert on gender equity in sport.

Nancy Hogshead, the superlative swimmer who claimed three golds and one silver at the 1984 L.A. Olympic Games. She later became an attorney and a very vocal advocate for women in sports. Today, Nancy serves as CEO of Champion Women, an organization that's pushing for equality and accountability in sports, and continues to build on the foundation established by our generation.

Pat McCormick, the American diver who swept both women's diving events at the 1952 and 1956 Summer Olympics — that's four gold medals over eight long years! She earned the James E. Sullivan Award for best amateur athlete in the U.S. in 1956 and was long my heroine. She broke so many boundaries in our sport and was involved at a critical period as diving began evolving from basic forms to more complicated maneuvers. The deeper I got into diving, the more she inspired me to push harder.

Picabo Street, a pioneering ski racer and media-savvy two-time Olympic medalist who hails from the appropriately named town of Triumph, Idaho. She hurtled down mountains so steep the view from the top is all but a dead-drop straight down — talk about having no fear! And as the first American to win a World Cup season title in a speed event, which she did in 1995, she helped bring downhill, slalom, and super G racing to prominence in the United States.

Sonja Henie, the three-time Olympic champion and 10-time World Champion figure skater from Norway who went on to become one of Hollywood's highest-paid stars in the 1930s. As a kid, I idolized her as I progressed through figure skating before figuring out diving was my true athletic calling.

★★★

I could continue for pages upon pages, but the point is, there are so many amazing women who have all pushed boundaries on behalf of women athletes.

As I sat in the stands watching these upcoming young divers perform, I found myself thinking back to JL LaMont and how lucky I was to meet him when I did. Had he not been the lifeguard at the Y, had he not said something to me about my "flips" off the diving board, I never would have ended up where I am. I would have missed seeing the world as I did and having the powerful experiences I had.

Along the way, a lot of things fell into place by accident, but there's more to being in the right place at the right time than sheer luck. You need to be able to take full advantage of unexpected opportunities whenever they happen. You need to be prepared for anything and be ready to step up when called on.

Just like in diving, everything in life is timing.

I enjoyed watching America's best divers show us their skills in Knoxville. And, I smiled as I breathed in the scent of chlorine and cheered as the Team USA 2024 Paris diving squad took shape. I look forward to seeing what these young people will achieve in the coming years, and I wonder what ground they may yet break for others.

All because of diving.

.

GLOSSARY OF TERMS

AAC: Founded in 1973, the Athletes' Advisory Council seeks to give Olympic athletes a voice and vote when it comes to matters that impact their participation in Olympic competitions.

AAU: Founded in 1888, the Amateur Athletic Union established standards and uniformity in amateur sports. Until the passage of Title IX in the 1970s forced the creation of more opportunities for women athletes, AAU competitions were the only option for women who wanted to compete and vie for an Olympic berth. Today, the AAU aims to serve all athletes at all levels of competition.

Approach: The forward steps a diver takes to reach the end of the diving board, preceding the hurdle and takeoff. The approach typically involves three or more steps.

Back dive: A group of dives that begins with the diver's back to the water and rotating away from the diving board.

Cliff diving: A type of diving that usually features very tall heights, often from a natural cliff or rock platform high above an open body of water.

Degree of difficulty: A number used to signify how technically challenging a specific dive is. The higher the DD, the more difficult and potentially dangerous the dive is. In diving, degrees of difficulty range from 1.2 to 4.1, and that number is multiplied by the sum of the judge's scores after the high and low scores are tossed out.

Entry: This is the conclusion of the dive and transpires when a diver makes contact with the water.

Forward dive: The diver starts facing the water and can use a standing or walking approach. The dive action is forward, away from the board, into the water.

Free position: Used in twisting dives, the free position is a combination of straight, pike, or tuck positions.

Hurdle: The diver takes forward steps to the end of the board and plants one foot about 12 inches from the end, while lifting the other knee and arms in preparation to land on both feet together at the end of the board. This allows divers to be balanced and ready for the board to launch them in the air as they execute their dives.

Inward dive: To execute an inward dive, divers stand at the end of the board with their back to the water and rotate toward the board.

Natatorium: The facility that houses the pool, diving well, and diving boards and towers. Typically, there are bleachers or stadium seating for spectators around the pool, with some deck space available for competitors, coaches, judges, and officials.

Olympic House: The USOC had a permanent headquarters in New York called Olympic House in the 1970s. This term can also refer to a hospitality venue set up for Team USA members during Olympic and Paralympic competitions, which is sometimes called Team USA House.

Pike position: To execute a pike, the diver bends the body at the hips with legs straight at the knees and toes pointed.

Platform: A diving platform is a 10-meter high structure from which "platform" diving events are performed. It is 33 feet off the water — the height of a three-story building. There is no spring off a 10-meter platform.

President's Commission on Olympic Sports: In 1975, President Gerald R. Ford established the PCOS in response to ongoing conflict among amateur sports organizations in the U.S. and declining performance by United States athletes in Olympic competition. The Commission's work eventually led to the passage of the Amateur Sports Act of 1978.

Reverse dive: Divers take off from a standing or running approach while facing the water, but the direction of rotation is toward the board.

Somersault: A circular rotation around the diver's horizontal axis. Somersaults can be a feature of any of the six categories of dive including forward, backward, reverse, inward, twisting, or armstand.

Springboard: An adjustable diving board that flexes to provide more height when the diver jumps. It is anchored to a structure about 10 feet (3 meters) above the surface of the water in Olympic diving. At the high school and collegiate levels, divers compete in the 1-meter springboard event.

Spotting rig: A training tool first developed by Dick Kimball that's now used in diving programs around the world to help athletes safely learn new dives with much reduced risk of injury. Spotting rigs are often used in conjunction with a dryland diving board, a trampoline, or gymnastics mats.

Straight: When in the straight position, the diver keeps the knees and hips straight with the feet together and toes pointed upon entry.

Synchronized diving: Tandem diving in which two divers perform the same dive at the same time, side by side. It became an Olympic sport in 2000, thanks in no small part to the efforts of Olympic bronze medalist and long-time diving administrator Tom Gompf.

Takeoff: When the diver leaves the board to execute a dive.

Title IX: The Sex Equity in Education Act, passed in 1975, intends to provide equal opportunities for women and men at all institutions of higher education in the United States. Better known by its nickname, Title IX, this law spans all areas of higher education, but is most closely associated with collegiate athletic programs.

Tower: The tall structure that houses diving boards. Platform diving is also sometimes referred to as tower diving because of the higher height of this discipline (10-meters in Olympic competition).

Tuck: In the tuck position, divers bring their knees and thighs close to the chest and the heels toward the buttocks so the body is in a tight ball.

Twisting dive: Any dive that features a twisting motion.

ABOUT THE AUTHORS

MICKI KING

Hailing from Pontiac, Michigan, Maxine "Micki" King showed an early aptitude for diving and attended the University of Michigan where she trained with legendary diving coach Dick Kimball. A top AAU competitor in the pre-Title IX era, King led the women's springboard diving event at the 1968 Mexico City Olympic Games when she hit her arm on the board during the 9th of 10 dives. With her left forearm fractured, she finished the contest in 4th place and assumed that was the end of her Olympic dream.

But as an officer in the U.S. Air Force, King was able to continue her love affair with diving. She qualified for the 1972 Olympic Games in Munich where she dominated the 3-meter springboard competition and claimed the gold medal that had eluded her four years prior.

After her Olympic success, King turned her attention to supporting other athletes, especially women, by helping pioneer the Athletes' Advisory Council. The AAC worked to give Olympic athletes a voice and vote going forward. Her involvement in supporting athletes' rights also led her to serve on the U.S. President's Commission on Olympic Sports (led by fellow Michigander President Gerald Ford) and pushing for the passage of the Amateur Sports Act of 1978.

King was a groundbreaker in many realms and was the first female staff member at the Air Force Academy in Colorado. There, she became the first woman to coach a male athlete to an NCAA title. She retired from the Air Force in 1992, having attained the rank of Colonel, and went on to serve as assistant athletic director at the University of Kentucky.

King gave back to diving and sports in general throughout her life via her work with the AAC, the Women's Sports Foundation, and as president of USA Diving from 1990 to 1994. She was inducted into the International Swimming Hall of Fame in 1978.

ELAINE K. HOWLEY

Elaine K. Howley is an award-winning freelance journalist and editor based in Boston, Massachusetts. A southern New Jersey native, Howley holds a bachelor's degree from Georgetown University and a master's degree in publishing and writing from Emerson College in Boston.

Specializing in sports, health, and history topics, Howley previously served as publications manager for U.S. Masters Swimming and managing editor of *SWIMMER* magazine. Her freelance work has appeared in *TIME, U.S. News & World Report,* AARP.org, *espnW,* and many others.

Her first book-length memoir ghostwriting project, *A Life Aloft,* completed with Tom Gompf and published by CG Sports Publishing in 2021, was awarded the 2023 Buck Dawson Authors Award from the International Swimming Hall of Fame.

www.ingramcontent.com/pod-product-compliance
Lightning Source LLC
Chambersburg PA
CBHW060419130626
46555CB00005B/2137